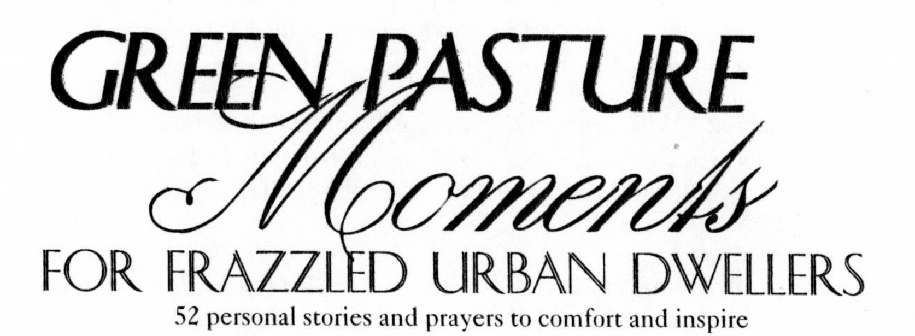

GLENDA-MAE GREENE, PH. D.

WITH CAROL J. GREENE, JANET M. GREENE, AND CHRISTINE A. GREENE

Printed in the United States of America

Publishing services by Selah Publishing Group, LLC, Arizona. The views expressed or implied in this work do not necessarily reflect those of Selah Publishing Group.

ISBN 1-58930-097-1
Library of Congress Control Number: 2003094192

52 personal stories and prayers to comfort and inspire

Dedication

This book is dedicated to my mother, Carol J. Greene, who tirelessly powered its fruition. Without her gentle prompting, these pages would have been reduced to a plethora of ideas swirling aimlessly in my head. Mom's courage, wisdom and supportive Christian faith formed the rudder beneath the sailboat of this dream. Carol Greene, the mother of three adult children and the grandmother of four, is one of the major co-authors of the book.

This book is also dedicated to the two other co-authors—my sister-in-law and my niece. Janet M. Greene is a cardiovascular nurse, pianist and avid photographer. Working as a team, she and her psychologist husband, home school their two daughters in central Florida.

Christine A. Greene is now in her second year of university. The story she included here was written when she was only 12. She plans to become a bilingual high school teacher wherever God sends her.

But this book is really dedicated to you, the reader, with our prayer that you will find perspective and comfort in its pages.

May God's peace-giving green pasture moments follow you all the days of your life.

Table Of Contents

Introduction

This devotional book is grounded on five realities:

1. That the beautiful Shepherd's psalm, Psalm 23, is laden with promises. It reminds us that our loving Shepherd-King pledges to be with us forever—at the beginning and end of every breath we take. He is always in control, whether we see it or not. He uses His staff to protect us, and His rod to correct us, if we let Him. Even though He knows every detail of our sinful lives, He still chooses to love us. We thrill to the intimate blessedness of David's opening line when transliterated from the Hebrew. "The Lord is the Shepherd of me." Accepting His offer is now up to us.
2. That Psalm 23 is the most comforting of all psalms. It is a poem-song of incredible beauty and hope. The soothing verses are among the first we memorized as children and the last we will whisper as we face our death. The Shepherd's Psalm is as relaxing as it is inspiring. Repeating its precious words in times of crisis often calms our frazzled nerves. This psalm is an onomatopoeic poem. Its meaning resides in both the sound and the pictures it inspires. We are just as reassured by the rhythm of its words as we are by the image of lush green pastures or peaceful streams. This poem-song is

the Book of Psalms in miniature; each thought or phrase portrayed in the six verses contains threads of congruence connecting it to the other psalms.

3. That every incident in our life experience can be framed with at least one of the promises of this beloved psalm, as the 52 stories in this volume illustrate. Like David, we sometimes sit in sumptuous splendor at His banquet table while we reflect on His promises. (*Open your mouth wide, and I will fill it with good things.* Ps. 81:10, NLT.) At other times we wreak vengeance on our enemies, if only in our thoughts. "*O God, declare them guilty. Let them be caught in their own traps.* Ps. 5:10, NLT). Too often we are reminded that our enemies are attitudes of our own choosing, attitudes that separate us from serving Him. (*I will not endure conceit and pride.* Ps. 101:5. NLT.)
4. That the power of the gospel parables and our own life stories is attributed to one simple fact: the shortest distance between the truth and the question is covered by a story. In much the same fashion, the easiest way to remember truth is through story.
5. That prayer, like reading the psalms, is a wonderful way of communing with God. It opens our hearts to God, drawing our minds closer to our heavenly Friend. Prayer gives us perspective on the joys and sorrows of our daily lives. When we come to God in humble, trusting faith, He can and will hear our prayer. He will let His light shine in our hearts.

As you riffle through the pages of this book, it is our prayer that hope, peace and comfort be yours.

May your Shepherd-Guide open your eyes to the pleasant green pasture moments found in each of your days.

The Shepherd's Psalm

The Lord is my shepherd;
I have everything I need.

He lets me rest in green meadows;
He leads me by peaceful streams.

He renews my strength.
He guides me along right paths,
bringing honor to His name.

Even when I walk through the dark valley of death,
I will not be afraid, for you are close beside me.
Your rod and staff protect and comfort me.

You prepare at a feast for me
In the presence of my enemies.
You welcome me as a guest,
anointing my head with oil.
My cup overflows with blessings.

Surely your goodness and unfailing love pursue me
All the days of my life,
And I will live in the house of the Lord
Forever.

New Living Translation

The Lord is my Shepherd

I Know The End Of The Story

The Lord is gracious and merciful,
Slow to anger and abounding in steadfast love.
The Lord is good to all,
And his compassion is over all that he has made.
Psalm 145:8,9, NRSV.

I remember the time I told my three-year-old niece the amazing story of Abraham's painful journey up Mount Moriah to sacrifice his beloved son, Isaac. As I described the father's breaking heart and the son's carefree enjoyment of the trip, her big brown eyes grew wide with wonder. When I recounted the moment when Abraham revealed the true purpose of the trek up the mountain, she held her breath.

Then I eagerly recounted the reprieve. A ram would take Isaac's place. To my surprise, I saw her lips quiver and two huge tears roll down her chubby cheeks. "Poor little ram," she sobbed. I had not expected her to hear the story from the ram's perspective, but the timing was perfect. Cuddling her on my lap, I explained the symbolism of the crucifixion story. Jesus was that little ram. He had to be killed so that we could live. I waited for the onset of fresh tears. Instead her eyes brightened, and she slid off my knee in search of her toys.

Bewildered, I asked her one question. "Why didn't you cry when I told you that Jesus had to die on the cross?"

"Because," she called from the other end of the room, "I know the end of the story. He's alive!" Her three-year old mind had grasped a concept my 40-something mind often ignores. In the battle against evil, we've already won!

No matter how treacherous the journey, how laborious the task of daily living, our Shepherd Savior guarantees victory.

My little niece reminded me that day that I have nothing to fear for the present if I remember that God has already deeded me a glorious future. Because of Him, we shall live. Like Job we can say, "But as for me, I know that my Redeemer lives, and that he will stand upon the earth at last." (Job 19:25, NLT).

I can but sing praises to God. I know the end of the story. He's alive!

Prayer For Today

Shepherd Guide,
You have freed me from the fear
of the dreaded unknown.
You have grounded me in Your steadfast truth.
You have granted me a salvation life,
and helped me live it.
Hallelujah!

Remind me each day that I know
the end of the story.
Your grace is sufficient for me.
You will shepherd me to life everlasting.
Hallelujah!
Amen

Just For You

Reproach has broken my heart,
and I am full of heaviness;
I looked for someone to take pity but there was none;
And for comforters, I found none.
They also gave me gall for food,
And for my thirst they gave me vinegar to drink.
Psalm 69:20.21, NKJV.

The businessman joined his wife at the medical center. They needed some pre-travel shots. She had an assignment in South America. He was accompanying her. "I'll let you go first," he told her, magnificent in his machismo. What he hoped was that the short delay would help him calm down. Then he watched as the nurse prepared the needle. For him. His pulse soared. His mouth grew dry. His palms sprouted tiny streams of moisture.

"Sir, would you like to sit down?" The all-seeing nurse was gentle as she poured him a cup of water. With a face as pale as parchment, he reached for the cup. "I'm fine," he croaked, more to convince himself than either the nurse or his waiting wife. His focus was on the encroaching needle.

But the nurse knew better. "Here," she offered, extracting a cherry-flavored lollipop—a treat usually reserved to comfort preschoolers. The eyes of that fifty-something professional lit up as he popped the sweet into his mouth. The flinching they all expected never happened. The ordeal was over. He had been comforted and emerged unscathed.

Listening to his wife recount the tale, I doubled over in mirth until he told her, "And I would do it again without the candy. Just for you."

I was struck by a vague similarity to another situation that neither of them could see at the moment. The businessman had sacrificed his manly pride so he could be with his wife on her South American mission trip. Our Shepherd-Savior sacrificed His life so that we could join Him in His celestial mansion. The man endured the momentary prick of a fearsome needle so that he could be with the woman who was utterly lovable in his eyes. Our Shepherd endured the horrendous press of a crown of thorns to redeem a people who seem totally unlovable.

There was no lollipop to mollify Him, just the sting of the scourging from the remorseless soldiers. Our text today (which we can also find in John 19:23) reminds us that there was no water for his parched lips, just the vinegar on a sponge that He had to refuse. There was no comforting loved one at His side, just the darkening of the heavens when God stepped back as His Son died for us.

Our Shepherd Savior died for us all, but He would have endured that excruciating agony just for me. Oh my loving Savior, I can never thank you enough.

Prayer For Today

Shepherd Redeemer,
You came down for me,
And I ignored You.
You suffered in agony alone.
And I despised You.
I broke Your heart,
Yet You died for me.
Oh my loving Savior,
I am so glad You're the Shepherd of me!
You live the promises that You speak.

No Pilot

This God is our God forever and ever;
He will be our guide even to the end.
Psalm 48:14, NIV.

One December my husband and I flew from sunny Florida to spend a wintry Christmas with our daughter in Michigan. Our son and his family would drive from Iowa to join us. I was looking forward to a white Christmas, the first one I'd experienced in many years. I knew that the warmth of family fellowship would be more than enough to counteract the frigid temperature.

We boarded the shuttle that was to take us to a small aircraft for the final leg of our journey. Then we just sat. The unusual delay in boarding the plane concerned us.

"You will have to go back to the terminal building. We have no pilot for this plane." A voice over the intercom instructed us, belatedly answering my spouse's question.

Stunned, we returned to the terminal. Later, we learned that there had indeed been a pilot, but he had already logged in his quota of hours for the day.

An hour later, with another pilot we boarded another plane only to hear him announce that there was a red light flashing on deck. "I don't know what that means," he told us. "But I know we won't take off until we get it checked."

"How long will we be delayed?" I wondered. It took three hours for the maintenance crew to rectify the problem and give the OK.

Thinking about our experience as the snowflakes frosted my mittens on my noonday walk the next day, I realized again that I had much for which to praise God. I was thankful that our safety had not been jeopardized. More than that, I was glad that our heavenly Pilot does not have a specified number of hours for His workday. Jesus, our Shepherd King never slumbers or sleeps. He is always prepared to guide us to the path to heaven.

There may be delays in our life paths as we stop to make repairs that we have necessitated, but God waits. He is always there to lead us to our final glorious destination. What a mighty God we serve!

Carol J. Greene

Prayer For Today

Thank you, ever-present Pilot.
You are ever beside me,
Every step of my way.
You have guided our generations throughout time.
You are changeless.

When we were rural,
You were our Shepherd.
Now we are urban,
You are our Pilot.
Yet Your plan remains the same.
You are always there to guide and bless us.
Every step of our way.

I will sing of Your mercy,
I will tell of Your goodness.
For You are God,
And I will serve You with gladness
Forever and ever.
Amen

I Have Everything I Need

YOU HAVE GOD

As the mountains surround Jerusalem,
So the Lord surrounds His people
From this time forth and forever.
Psalm 125:2, NRSV.

The lunch table was cleared and we moved to the living room, engaged in desultory conversation. Soon it was time for everyone to leave. As the goodbyes began, the doorbell rang. A bright-eyed four-year-old in a flurry of petticoats and pigtails, burst into the room. "Where is my grandma?" she wanted to know.

"I'm right here, sweetheart." My friend enveloped the little girl in a hug only grandmothers can give.

"Well, let's go." Her hand firmly clasping her grandmother's, the child strode to the door, beginning the exodus of all the other guests.

"But how can you take her away?" I asked in mock despair. "I'll be all alone." My mournful tone was doing nothing to change the child's decision.

"You have God," she reminded me. "That is enough." With that she escorted her beloved grandparent to the waiting car.

Later that afternoon as I walked down to the lake nearby, I realized anew that my little friend was right. I was surrounded by God. I saw Him in His eye for color in the ruby red of the fall dogwoods. He appeared in the apricot kiss of the setting sun reflecting on the water. I heard Him in the glorious evening birdsong. I tasted Him in the tangy crunch of the apple from my neighbor's orchard. I felt Him in the cooling breezes that caressed my cheek. Yes, I had God and He was more than enough.

Meditating on His goodness on the waterfront park bench, I turned the pages of my mind's catalogue of blessings. God was my environment. And it was good. Everything was charged with His grandeur.

Now it is my turn to act out my thanks for the bounties of life. With David I must say, *"I'll be the poet who sings your glory—and lives what I sing every day"* (*Ps. 61:8. The Message*). I cannot help but reflect the God-life as I experience His Word and live it.

Prayer For Today

Creator of the Universe,
I cannot praise You enough for Your blessings,
Your wisdom,
Your creatures, great and small.

Thank you for little children
Who remind me that
I have need of nothing.
Because I have You, gracious God.
It is more than enough.
Amen

There's No Such Thing As Only

The Lord is like a father to His children,
Tender and compassionate to those who fear Him.
For He understands how weak we are.
Psalm 103:13 & 14, NLT.

She was only a little girl, whisked away from her parents by a band of marauding warriors. Left alone to struggle with fright, homesickness, and the stench of leprosy in her new home, she could have heaped criticism on her new master's head. In a blaze of tears, she could have said to herself, "Serves him right. That's what happens when you abduct innocent children." She could have, but she didn't. She could have reasoned, "I'm just a little slave girl. I'm too young and too new to be helpful here." She could have, but she didn't. Instead she made a single health-restoring suggestion. "If only my master were with the prophet who is in Samaria! For he would heal him" (2 Kings 5:3, NKJV).

Two short sentences, wistful yet accurate. The pathos and the power of those words must have moved her mistress to action. After all the learned doctors, all the anguish, all the failed treatments, here it was: the diagnosis and the cure in one small voice.

The little girl could have left the telling to someone older or wiser than she. But she resolved to share the message of hope herself with the help of her God. And the Shepherd of little lambs saw the workings of faith in this young girl. She had no money, no status, no special ability, or so it seemed. Yet God used her to lead the captain of a great army to exclaim, "Now I know that there is no God in all the world except Israel" (2 Kings 5:15, NIV).

He was only a small boy, bringing to the Master's preachin the lunch his mother had lovingly prepared. When Andrew asked for his food, he could have said, "You adults know how long these meetings run. Plan ahead." He could have, but he didn't.

He could have said, “No, I’m too young to share; too young to starve.” But he didn’t. He could have suggested a compromise, “I’ll keep one barley loaf and a fish, and you can have the rest.” He could have, but he chose not to. Willingly, he turned over the basket to the disciple. And there in Mark 6, we find the recipe for a miracle.

To five barley loaves,
And two small fish,
Add one small boy with a big heart.
Wrap it in the touch of the Master’s hand.

Yield: Lunch for 5,000 (15, 000 if you approximate for families).

With that lunch and the Christ’s touch, hundreds of hungry listeners were fed. Sometimes when God performs miracles, He uses someone quiet enough and little enough to do great things for Him. All we need is trust. He is everything we need.

God said as much to the youthful Jeremiah in about 620 B.C. “Do not say, ‘I am only a child.’ You must go to everyone I send you to and say whatever I command you. Do not be afraid of them, for I am with you.” (Jeremiah 1:7, 8, NIV.) There is no such thing as only when we work through Him.

Prayer For Today

If You used little children then,
Compassionate Lord,
Please use me now.
Remind me that when I am with You,
I have need of nothing.
Amen

I Told Jesus He Could Change My Name

As your name deserves, O God,
You will be praised to the ends of the earth.
Psalm 48:10, NLT.

Our names are important to us, perhaps because we feel they embody a particular aspect of our personality, or because they have special meaning. Sometimes names reflect a family history. I have friends whose names are distinctive because they are a legacy from a significant other—mother, grandmother, teacher, doctor—or a significant place. On the other hand, my cousin Avonie loves her name because no one else seems to have had it before she did. It makes her feel unique.

I like my own name because my mother once told me how she selected it and what she hoped it would mean for me. She wanted me to be "a brilliant, resilient and sensitive person growing up under the shadow of God's love."

When my brothers and I were quite small, our grandmother offered to pay $1000 (a gigantic sum at that time) to the first one of us who named his/her first daughter Hephzibah. Not understanding the context for that name in Isaiah 62, we all flatly refused. We only knew that the name was unfamiliar to our tongues. It took me years to discover the glorious meaning of the name—delight of God.

It's a joy to read the Bible, paying particular attention to the meaning—implicit or explicit—of names. I particularly enjoy reading those passages when angels appear to expectant mothers and name their children, giving them special significance. In my mind's eye, I see mothers nurturing the genius of those special children, instilling in them the spirit to accomplish the purpose for which they were called. Samuel, "gift from God." Barnabas, "son of encouragement."

Even more precious to me, though, are the passages that document a renaming for people who had a change of heart. Their new names broadcast to the world a pristine focus. From Jacob to Israel, "father of nations"; from Saul, vengeance-wreaking zealot, to Paul, "dynamic evangelist."

Names, no matter how beautiful, are never as important as the persons who are called by them, or the expectations they fulfill in the heart of God. As we grow to recognize that our Shepherd has a purpose for each of us, we will get excited in that knowledge. If I had to choose another name for myself now, I really think I would select Hephzibah. My grandmother was right! I want to be a "delight of the Lord." More importantly, I want to be what He wants me to be. That is my delight.

There is, however, no name as important as God's name. Let us give Him the praise, obedience and honor He deserves.

Prayer For Today

I am excited, gentle Shepherd,
By my new name, Delight of the Lord.
I am honored by the legacy inherent in the name.
I want to be Your delight.
I want to walk in Your footsteps.
Because of You, I have everything I need.

Thank You, Redeemer God,
For a new name and a new heart.
Give me grace and courage
To reflect Your heart,
And nothing but Your goodness.
And I will be careful to give You all the praise.
Because of You, I have everything I need.
Amen

He Lets Me Rest In Green Meadows

Lesson From A Pale Pink Rose

Praise the Lord, I tell myself;
O Lord my God, how great you are!
You cause plants to grow for people to use.
Psalm 104:1&14, NLT.

Carla came into the office for her weekly counseling session. The usual smile was on her lips, but her cheeks were tear-smudged. The therapist could see the pain, but Carla said nothing.

Eventually she could hold it no longer. "My daughter Kayla is having problems at school. The substitute teacher accused her of cheating because she got a perfect score on her math test. My Kayla loves math. She's good at it but she walked out of that classroom in despair. She came home so broken, so discouraged, so—"Words failed and tears threatened.

The counselor made a mental note to call the school to see if she could intervene. Two days passed and, unsure of what strategies to employ, the woman still had done nothing. But before the week ended Carla was back. There was a glow in her eyes, and the spring was back in her stride. "I had the most wonderful experience yesterday!" She almost sang the words. And she proceeded to talk about the all-night prayer session she had had with her God. "Then He gave me an idea," she bubbled.

Going to the nearest flower shop, Carla had purchased a pale pink rose that had just started to open. She took it to the school that noon and offered the flower to the substitute teacher. "You see this rose?" Carla set the tone for the dialogue. "This is my daughter. I think she is special. Like this rosebud, she is fragile. We have to treat roses very carefully."

She was about to develop her metaphor further, but the teacher got the point immediately. Misty-eyed, she admitted her distress at the words she had carelessly uttered. Right after lunch, she apologized to Kayla and then to the entire class.

A smiling Kayla bounced through the door that late afternoon, sharing with her mother the joys of the school day. Then she settled down to finish her math homework. All this because of the prayer-filled gift of a single pale pink rose. God never promised us a walk through a thornless rose garden, but He promised a walk to a sure destination. And He will be with us always as loving protector and guide.

There are some things that only God can fix. We need to learn to stand back and watch Him work. God taught me that lesson that day. I know. Because I was that counselor!

Prayer For Today

Heavenly Shepherd,
Thank You for simple things—
For silence,
For pain,
For beautiful rosebuds,
And the wisdom to use them.
As I glory in the joy of watching You work,
I have to say again,
Thank You Lord, for everything.
Amen

Uh-Oh

Praise the Lord, I tell myself,
And never forget the good things he does for me.
He forgives all my sins,
And surrounds me with love and tender mercies.
He fills my life with good things
His salvation extends to those who
are faithful to his covenant.
Psalm 103:2, 3, 4, 5, 15, NLT.

When I developed a problem with my shoulder, weeding in my flower garden became a rather difficult task. Because I thought the next day would show some improvement in my flexibility, I left the weeding for the next day, and the next. Stubbornly, I refused to tell anyone about my dilemma or employ a gardener. All too soon the weeds took over. I promised myself I'd take care of the situation 'tomorrow.'

Early one evening, I came home to find my next-door neighbor weeding my garden. She had her little daughter with her. Parking the car in the garage, I swallowed my embarrassment and went to the front door to greet the duo. But before I could get there, the doorbell sounded. It was my little neighbor.

"Uh-oh," she said woefully. She held up one of my prized Queen of the Night tulips, bulb and all. "Uh-oh," she said again, golden eyes darkening in her distress.

Her mother came rushing over to apologize, "I'm so sorry," she said. "We noticed that you'd been so busy lately that you didn't seem to have time to pull the weeds. Since I had some time, I thought I'd help out a bit. Our daughter wanted to help too, but she hasn't learned the difference between flowers and weeds yet." She brushed the dirt from her child's pants. "I'm so sorry," she said again.

Looking out on my garden the next day, I knew I'd trade more than a single prize tulip for wonderful neighbors and a weed-free garden any day. Apologies were totally unnecessary.

That incident was a graphic reminder that I have a similar choice in life. I must choose between weeds or tulips. Weeds unchecked take over the garden. Sins unchecked take over our lives.

One of my favorite authors, Ellen G. White, once wrote. "When faith in God's word is lost, the soul has no safeguard" (*Christ's Object Lessons* [Silver Spring, MD: Better Living Publications, 1990], p. 9).

How will you safeguard the garden of your heart from the encroaching weeds of sin? Our Shepherd-Gardener is standing by, patiently waiting for our decision. He loves to be our safeguard. Don't put it off till tomorrow.

Prayer For Today

Shepherd-Gardener, I will never forget
The good things You do for me.
Thank you for helping as I weed out my sins.
I will safeguard my soul with Your word.
Thank you for Your extravagant blessings.

Stand beside me and surround me
With Your tender mercy.
Thank You for the verdant lushness of
Your peaceful meadows.
I will praise Your name today.
I will leave nothing that important for tomorrow.
I must praise Your name today.
Amen

Love Letters From My Backyard

"Because he loves me," says the Lord,
I will rescue him; I will protect him,
For he acknowledges my name."
Psalm 91:14, NIV.

Even though I am a horrible correspondent myself, I love getting letters. The advent of e-mail a decade ago improved my communication patterns. Somewhat. But it is not the same as a brilliantly humorous card a friend would craft, or the affection-laden scrawl of that special someone.

One frosty evening, as my trek to the mailbox garnered nothing but bills or notices addressed to "Current Resident," I groused to the star-splattered sky, "All I ask is one letter."

The next morning, curled up in an overstuffed armchair next to the window overlooking the backyard, I saw my first love letter. Two bright red cardinals were perched on a snow-laden tree. I had never seen them so close before. God had sent a love letter to me. And then I realized that I had been getting letters all along but never once picked them up.

Now I see them everywhere. In every season.

In the spring,
the roses covering the thorns,
the protective doe with her fawn in the distance,
His love embraces me

In the summer,
the ruby-throated hummingbird sipping nectar from the daylilies,
the sweet succulence of ripe peaches plucked from the tree,
His love enchants me.

In the fall,
the fruity fragrance of neighboring vineyards,
brilliant chrysanthemums shouting His glory,
His love sustains me.

In the winter,
blankets of snow decorating the evergreens,
branches extended to help me navigate steep paths,
His love supports me.

In people,
the spontaneous toothless grin of my baby niece when I cuddle her in a fond embrace,
the infectious chuckle of my pre-teen neighbor as she shares watermelon, green peppers, and her brand of wisdom,
the gentle, unsolicited kiss from my 'tween-aged nephew,
His love exalts me.

In His Word year round,
"See how great a love the Father has bestowed upon us, that we should be called children of God, and such we are." (I John 3:1, NASB).
His love humbles me.

Prayer For Today

Thank You, loving Lord,
I know You love me.
Your love letters encircle my soul.
Open my eyes so that I can see them.
Open my heart so that I can feel them.
Open my arms so that I can share them.
I owe everything to You.
And I love You.
Amen

He Leads Me By Peaceful Streams

Duckling In Distress

I looked for some to take pity, but there was none;
And for comforters, but I found none.
They gave me gall for my meat; and in my thirst they
gave me vinegar to drink. Psalm 69: 20, 21, NKJV.

We sauntered along the expansive green lawns of Edwards gardens in Toronto one sunny afternoon. The stately trees and brilliant blossoms reminded us that we were reading a page from God's second book—nature. Traversing the curving paths, we came upon a bridge that spanned a stream. I noticed idly that the brook flowed over a series of small steps. As my cousin leaned over to look for the giant gold fish for which the beautiful park was famous, a duck and eight fluffy ducklings came into view.

The mother duck sailed down the steps, obviously quacking instructions to her little ones. The first one made it over the steps. So did the second one, and the third. But the fourth duckling seemed petrified. It kept swimming around in frenzied circles, clucking woefully.

The mother duck turned around. Unable to brave the current and move back up the steps, she quacked even louder. The other ducklings moved over the steps successfully. Duckling number four, however, could not descend. With a final call, one of farewell perhaps, the mother and her seven babes began swimming away.

And then we heard a splash. A tow-headed little boy, with unchallenged optimism, had jumped into the shallow stream to rescue the frightened bird. Very gently, he returned it to the flock. The onlookers cheered while his parents shook their heads in bemused wonderment. The six-year-old, his pants and sandals soaking wet, bowed. He had been the duckling's messiah.

I reflected on that remarkable scene for days. For the young lad, the rescue was a relatively risk-free adventure that brought nothing but good for the duckling, and a sense of altruistic satisfaction for himself. For our Jesus, His mission brought everything glorious to us, and everything painful—God-separated, soul-wrenching agony—to Him.

The apostle Peter explains it beautifully. "*For you know that God paid a ransom to save you from the empty life you inherited from our ancestors. He paid for you with the precious lifeblood of Christ, the sinless, spotless Lamb of God. (I Peter 1:18, 19, NLT).*

While the boy's clothes were simply splashed with water, our Lord's clothes were streaked with jagged stains of His own blood as He bore the soldiers' angry scourging in quiet anguish. But the saddest of all comparisons is this: while the youngster's mission was greeted with cheers, jeers bade the Messiah farewell.

Prayer For Today

Gentle Shepherd,
Thank You for rescuing me.
I am blessed by your sacrifice.
I am comforted by Your guidance.
I am amazed by Your love.
Oh my loving Savior,
I can never thank You enough
For saving me.
Amen

Ivory Keys

Who are those who fear the Lord?
He will show them the path they should choose.
Psalm 25:12, NLT.

My two little granddaughters came to visit me one afternoon. They made their customary rounds, pausing only briefly to examine the ceramic doll, recline on the lounger, and use the speakerphone. Then they gravitated to the piano. The older one takes lessons, so we could recognize her music without difficulty when she manipulated the ivory keys. When the younger one joined in, however, cacophony ensued.

Sitting beside the two small bodies, I set the boundaries for their keyboarding exploration. The younger one got the octaves above middle C, the older one got the keys below that note. My strategy worked wonderfully—for about three minutes. And then I heard the distress call.

"Grandma," the older one called. "She's playing on my side."

"Sweetheart," I chided the younger virtuoso, "you must remember to stay one your side. If you both want to play, you have to follow the rule. If you can't play together, then you can't play at all." With the problem solved, I returned to the kitchen to fix supper.

A minute later I was surprised to see a little pink-clad cherub marching determinedly to another room. Then with the insight grandmothers are supposed to have developed when they attain that venerated status, I came to understand her nonverbal line of reasoning. She had chosen peace at her price. She had been given a choice. She had made a decision. She was acting out the consequences. It wasn't the decision I wanted her to make, but I had to respect her choice, even though she was not quite two.

Our Heavenly Father also respects our choices. He will not force us to choose His way. Instead He lovingly bids us follow Him. What will your choice be today?

Carol J. Greene

Prayer For Today

I choose peace, Father.
The peace that passes all understanding.
The peace of silent waters
In the cacophony of life.
Guide me as I glide over the ebony and ivory keys of today's struggles.
Show me the way, Father.
Your way.
I choose You.
I choose peace.
Amen

Look What I've Got!

Though its waters roar and be troubled,
Though the mountains shake with its swelling,
There is a river whose streams
shall make the city of God glad.
The Lord of hosts is with us.
Psalm 46:3,4, 7, NKJV.

My mother heard a tapping at her bedroom window one morning. "Why would the workmen from the house next door use the window instead of the door to get my attention?" she asked me as she went to investigate the reason for the unusual commotion. Instead of construction workers, however, she saw a large sandhill crane pecking at her windowpane!

The stately bird's bald ruby crown glistened in the sunlight as it stretched its long neck upwards to a height of almost five feet. "Rat-tat-tat. Tat." The pecking started again. "If this had happened at night and I hadn't seen the bird, my heart would have stopped," my mother told me. She had a point. The sound of that long black bill rapping against the windowpane was eerily human. My heart would have stopped too.

"Rat-tat-tat. Tat. Tat." The knocking started again as the bird moved to another window. My eyes followed its bustle-like rear as it stalked, stiletto legged, through the backyard. I could see his mate several yards away, lowered head searching for food by the pine trees. Beside her was the reason for the disturbance. Two tiny clumps of strawberry blond down with the unmistakable shape of their parents were climbing down the ridge to their nest by the canal. Proud papa bird had been trying to say, "Look what I have!"

The adult birds were familiar members of our community. I had first seen them, standing sentinel-like, at the gate, when we first explored the community. I had seen them again when they welcomed us back from Alaska in the summer. Now I was seeing them as a complete family.

I thought about that precious moment for weeks. Eventually I found the spiritual parallel imbedded in it. The cranes had been giving me a thumbnail sketch of the principles of witnessing. They taught me three powerful lessons.

First, like the adult birds, we must make ourselves known to our community as positive witnesses before we start to share God's love. Then, we have to be passionate about the message we are sharing. And finally, we must never get discouraged. Like father bird, we may need to try several avenues before the message gets though. But we must keep spreading the Word. It is too important to keep to ourselves.

Prayer For Today

Thank You, Creator of birds that nest on the
banks of gentle streams,
For showing us that there is
Quietude in the clamor of nature,
That there is peace to be found in everything.

Lead us through Your second book.
Let us see Your love and glory.
Teach us to know You.

Help us to learn Your truth
And be comforted.
Show us how to share Your truth,
And rejoice by the river
Whose streams make the City of God glad
Because You, the Lord of hosts, are with us.
Amen

He Renews My Strength

I Am Somebody

O God, don't stay way,
Please hurry to help me.
Bring disgrace and destruction
on those who accuse me.
May humiliation and shame
cover those who want to harm me.
I will tell everyone about your righteousness.
All day long I will proclaim your saving power,
For I am overwhelmed by how much
you have done for me.
Psalm 71: 12, 13, 15, NLT.

They were right, of course. I was not supposed to be with him, but I felt powerless. I could not refuse his advances. Circumstances seemed to offer me neither escape nor strength. Looking back at that dismal day, I know that these words sound like mere excuses. I am sure I could have found a way out, but I didn't.

As it was, they caught us. Rough hands dragged me out into the streets. I did not even have a moment to straighten my robe. Then I heard those conniving Pharisees interrupt the gentle Jesus who was teaching a crowd in the temple courts.

"Teacher," they reported. "This woman was caught in the very act of adultery. In the law Moses commanded us to stone such women. Now what do you say?"

I understood then that they had plotted *my* downfall all along. I was nothing but a pawn in their terrible strategy. Of course, my partner—if that is what you'd call him—was nowhere in sight. What else could I have expected? I had always been mistreated, overlooked, spat upon, abused and talked about. I was a nothing in their eyes. A nobody even in my own eyes.

I knew that Pharisees whispering behind me were eagerly awaiting His answer. In disgrace, I cowered on the sandy ground, waiting for the first rock. The moments dragged by. Nothing happened.

Peeping through my drooping eyelids, I watched the Master stoop. The Pharisees moved in to harass Him further. I could not see what was happening, but a hush fell over the crowd. And then I saw Him writing with His finger in the dust. I could not see what He was writing. But I saw when He stood up.

"Let anyone among you who is without sin be the first to throw the stone at her."

I knew my time had come. Closing my eyes, I waited for my stoning. But nothing happened. In disbelief, I watched the men, every one of them, slink away in disgrace. They had been caught in a trap of their own making, convicted of sins I was never to know about. Sins written on the sand that a gentle puff of wind erased.

But I could not leave. This was my only chance to linger in the presence of Infinite Purity; my only glimmer of hope. But I could not look at Him. Then He spoke, "Woman, has no one stayed to accuse you?"

There was no one left—just the Master and me. And then I heard the most melodious sound I have ever heard. It was His voice, speaking two precious sentences. "Then neither do I condemn you," Jesus declared. "Go now and leave your life of sin." (John 8:11, NIV.)

I had not lost my future. Weights crumbled like sand shapes from my shoulders. My fear turned to faith. I was renewed. He had changed my life path from destruction to distinction. They had dragged in on a nightmare, but He sent me out with a vision. He had set me free. Now I know that I am somebody. With His help, I can change the world.

Prayer For Today

Thank You, gentle Jesus,
For reminding me of the majestic power
Of a single sweep of Your grace-filled fingers,

When I cannot see Your face,
I can trace Your hand.
Though You carved the Law in stone,
You scribbled my sins in dust,
And a single puff of the midday breeze
Can blow all traces of them away.

Thank You, dear Lord,
For saving me,
For loving me,
For restoring me.

I will tell everyone
That You are just and good.
Because of You,
I am somebody.
Help me change the world today.
Amen

A Stronger Arm

Now I know that the Lord saves the anointed.
He will answer him from his holy heaven
With the saving strength of his right arm.
Psalm 20:6 NKJV.

I love being a grandmother. Living only six miles away from my two youngest granddaughters and watching them grow brings me much pleasure and pride. Perhaps it is because I've gone over this road before and know the pitfalls to avoid; or perhaps it is because I know that the total responsibility of rearing them is not mine alone. Whatever the reason, when I discover that I have to pick the girls up from school, it is impossible to wipe the smile from my lips.

On this particular Tuesday afternoon, the eight-year-old decided she wanted to try a recipe she had found on the Internet. Gravely collecting all the items from her handwritten recipe, she fetched a mixing bowl and a wooden spoon. Then she asked me, "Grandma, please preheat the stove." I was her willing assistant.

Soon I could see the little head bent industriously over the bowl. It was as if she were talking to herself with each stroke. "I will make brownies. They will be good. My mom will like them. My big sister will like them. Even the neighbors will want a sample."

Then I watched as her strokes slowed and finally stopped. "Grandma," she called. "This is hard. I need a stronger arm. Can you help me?" Again I was her willing assistant.

Even at her tender age, Briana seemed to know that her success in baking demanded teamwork. She could not do it alone.

Munching on the child's tasty treat that evening, I thought of the similarities between our relationship and the one I shared with my heavenly Father. We are a team. My success in any endeavor is based on how closely I work with Him. I know He delights in my company. He has told me that on several occasions. I read it in today's text, in Psalm 100:5 and Isaiah 43:3. I know He is always willing to help me. But what is most significant is that His is the stronger arm in our partnership. I must always remember that as I delight in His presence.

Carol J. Greene

Prayer For Today

Thank You, dear God, for Your promise.
Regardless of the size of my need,
I know that I am
Always on Your mind,
And in Your hand.
Remind me to ask for Your assistance
in everything I do.
Help me to remember the saving sweetness
Of Your strength.
Always.
Amen

Perfection In Progress

He who walks in a perfect way,
He shall serve me.
Psalm 101:6, NKJV.

"Will you look at this?" The young mother asked, distress resonating in soprano. Reaching for the crumpled paper, her husband scanned the scribbles on display. A frown marred his handsome face. This was a homework assignment their son intended to hand in to the teacher! Then the muscles in his face relaxed in a moment of insight. "What we have here is perfection in progress," he observed. "The failures are crossed out. The first thoughts revised. And look here," he said, pointing to the holes in the paper. "The lad tried so hard to erase his mistakes that the paper disappeared. But the answers are all correct. Apparently that is *his* bottom line."

Violetta thought about it for a moment. It made sense. To a point. "But does he have to hand it in like this? Can't he rewrite it? I wouldn't accept it myself. How can he expect his teacher to take it?"

"Be that as it may," her husband continued, "priority setting, not error making seemed to be at issue here. Our son only left himself a limited amount of time for the assignment to be completed. Hence this crumpled paper. Things like this will happen once in a while."

"From now on, we shall have to concentrate on helping him decide what comes first," Violetta agreed. "I'll help him manage his time. He really has to learn to put first things first." Her tone was decisive.

I suspect that is how our Shepherd Redeemer intervened in Rahab's behalf and brought her to the veneration implicit in Hebrews 11:31. I know that is how He works on my behalf. I may try to scrub the memory of my sins away. To no avail. The blood of Christ erases all my faults. I am forgiven. God hands me a clean page. He will help me put first things first.

When He was on earth, Jesus always viewed people from the perspective of their potential. He saw the latent ability of the Samaritan woman at the well, and conscripted her to evangelistic service. "Go tell others," He said. (John 4:16). He did the same for the unfocused and seemingly spineless Peter when He promoted him to "fisher of men" (Matthew 4:19).

What divine perception. What a Savior! Through Him perfection is more than a possibility. It's a promise!

Prayer For Today

Gentle Shepherd, You bring me such hope.
You cleared my sin-scarred page
With Your blood.
You bring me such promise.
You called me to Your kingdom.
You bring me such love.
I will put You first in all things.
I will serve You
Forever.
Amen

He Guides Me Along Right Paths

Confusion In The Parking Lot

I [the Lord] will instruct you and teach you
in the way you should go;
I will counsel you with my eye upon you.
Psalm 32:8, AMP.

One winter evening I drove a friend to the airport to catch the last flight to Chicago. Pulling in to the parking lot, I glanced at my watch. We had 15 minutes to spare. He grabbed his duffel bag, and I picked up his briefcase. Together we rushed to the departure gate. Suddenly, he stopped short. He had left his ticket in the car.

"Give me the keys," he urged. "I'll race back and get it."

"The car's not locked," I reminded him, and he dashed off.

A few minutes later he returned, shaking his head. "The car *is* locked." I knew it wasn't, but there was no time to debate the issue. I handed over the keys. He came back shortly after with ticket in hand and a rueful grin on his face. "I was trying to get into the wrong car," he admitted.

After the plane took off, I walked back to the parking lot. There were indeed two black Cherokees parked side by side. But the differences were obvious—to me. "How could he have made that mistake?" I asked the cold moonlit night. "The other car is brand-new. It has neither the dents nor rust bubbles that decorate my jeep. Mine has gold-colored running boards; the other one doesn't."

As I listed the differences, I remembered that a similar thing had happened to me several months earlier. I, too, had tried to get into someone else's car, simply because one the same size and color as the one I had rented was parked in the same area. There are differences, it finally occurred to me, that are obvious only to full-time owners. Especially at first glance.

Sometimes as we rush along on life's journey, we become confused by spiritual look-alikes. Our Creator and Redeemer will never be confused. He made each one of us, numbering the very hairs on our heads. Then He redeemed us with His blood. He knows the difference. Now it is our turn to really get to know *Him*.

Prayer For Today

Redeemer God,
Thank You for Your loving watchcare.
You know what makes us unique.
You created us.
And then You saved us.
You did not say,
"I'll show you the way."
You said instead,
"I am the way."
Please keep Your eyes upon us
As we voyage on life's pathway.
Guide us,
And grant us wisdom, peace and safety.
Help us to learn to know You,
The only true God.
Amen

1741 Hill

Show me the path where I should walk, O Lord;
Point out the right road for me to follow.
Psalm 24:4, NLT.

Looking in the mirror one Thursday afternoon, I knew that it was time to take advantage of the 20% off coupon my stylist had sent, inviting me to visit her at a new location. I had to make a series of presentations that weekend and could not allow my unruly hairstyle to distract the audience.

Checking the address for the new salon, 1741 Hill, I sallied forth. The after-work traffic was just beginning to build up as I turned on to Hill Street. Slowing down to search for the number, a cavalcade of cars started honking their impatience behind me. I had not yet found the number, but I moved on regardless.

Doubling back I looked for the number again. To no avail. Parking in an office parking lot, I reached for my cane, determined to find the salon on foot. Hobbling down the road, I checked the numbers on the block. There was no such number. Finally I went into an office. "I can't seem to find 1741 Hill. Can you tell me where to find it?" I asked the gentleman behind the desk.

"Oh, madam," he said courteously. "This is Hill Street. You must be looking for 1741 Hill Avenue. It's about two miles down the road."

An hour later with hair neatly coiffed, I collapsed, exhausted, on my sofa. I realized that I had made one major mistake. I had not put first things first. I did not have the complete address before I set off on my journey. In essence, I did not know where I was going and had wasted both time and energy in finding the location. A line from John Newton's often-sung hymn came to mind. "I once was lost. But now am found." And I, thinking that the salon was nowhere to be found, had been totally unaware that I was the one who was lost!

Perhaps it had only been because I felt intimated by the pressure of impatient drivers behind me, or because of the ache in my tightening muscles that I asked that one vital question. But was I ever so glad that I asked! Some sage once opined, "If you don't know where you're going, you'll probably end up some place else." He was right.

As the spiritual connection between that experience and my spiritual journey became clear, I fell to my knees in prayerful penitence. "I am totally lost without You, dear God. I ask Your guidance in everything I do. Please inscribe Your directions on my heart. I will put You first in everything."

Had the expedition been worth it? The mirror suggested that it had been. And so, much more, did my grateful heart.

Prayer For Today

Thank You, Merciful God for that reminder.
I will make You first in my life.
I will ask the right questions.
Help me to begin every journey
With Your directions engraved on my heart.
Point out the way that I should go.
Remind me that I am totally lost without You.
You are my way.
I will ask Your guidance.
Lead, gentle Shepherd and I will follow.
And that is my promise.
Amen

Message In Ivy Leaves

Your testimonies are wonderful;
Therefore my soul keeps them.
The entrance of your words gives light;
It gives understanding to the simple.
Psalm 119:129,130, NKJV.

In the throes of completing the final chapters of my dissertation some years ago, I hit a metaphorical logjam. The thoughts that flooded my brain were jumbled. The words seemed meaningless. Taking a break, I did what most of my girlfriends would do in a similar situation—I cleaned my kitchen. I mopped the floor, scrubbed the stove, cleaned the oven, and washed the curtains. Convinced I had breached the impasse, I returned to my computer, but my thoughts were still confused. I resorted to doing more laundry, focusing on linen this time.

Lifting a pot of trailing ivy from the lace covering of a small round table, I noticed that the delicate cloth was attached to the earthen jar. Tugging gently at the cloth I intended to launder, I saw that two ivy fronds had worked their way into the spaces of the crocheted material and grown healthy leaves. Reluctant to break off the tender young shoots, I lowered the vase back to the table.

Staring down at the plant, sprawled as gracefully as cursive on the tiny table, I searched for the spiritual metaphor I am sure is embedded in each of our life experiences. At first I could make no connection with the lustrous green and ivory leaves curled in elegant disarray across the table. Then I saw the link. God had written me an elegant note in ivy leaves.

Isaiah's words sprang to mind. "See, I have written your name on my hand. Ever before me is a picture of Jerusalem's walls in ruins."(Isa. 49:16, NLT). It was as if my heavenly Editor had sent me a memo in ivy-leafed script. The walls of my disjointed literary style were about to come down.

Infused with the wonder of God's glory, I returned to my keyboard. In the hours that sped by on angels' wings, I noted that my thoughts flowed freely, the transitions were clear, and the analysis creatively cogent. The wall—my stylistic logjam—was literally in ruins. His words had given light to this simple mind.

When I flew to Seattle to accept the outstanding dissertation award from a rather prestigious research society, I was reminded again that everything that happens, even the writing of a paltry paper, is part of our Father's concern. He had guided me yet again.

Prayer For Today

You, O Lord, are as wonderful as Your word—
And that we know is outstanding.
I am infused with the wonder of Your glory.
Remind me that You are the Guide.
As You direct my paths—metaphorical
or spiritual,
Lead, Precious Shepherd,
I will follow.
You are my way.
You are the only way.
Amen

Even When I Walk Through The Dark Valley of Death

A Circle Of Glory

I will sing your praises among the nations.
For your unfailing love is higher than the heavens.
Your faithfulness reaches to the clouds.
Psalm 108:3,4, NLT.

My father needed surgery—a rather complicated operation that the doctors had scheduled immediately. I quickly booked a flight to Orlando to be with my parents at the appointed time. My job, or so I imagined, was to hold my mother's hand, bring a smile to my father's face, and keep my brothers in phone contact.

"Who'll be there for you?" my friends worried.

"I'm strong," I assured them, settling the mantel of self-confidence securely on my shoulders.

During the flight that rain-swept afternoon, the pilot advised us that he was flying high above the clouds to avoid the impending storm. Idly I looked out the window. It was then that I spotted the most fantastic sight I had ever seen. I blinked. They were still there. Reaching for the glasses I rarely wore in public, I noted that the beautiful blend of colors were even clearer. There on the cottony clouds were two brilliant rings of light in the seven colors of the rainbow.

Those ovals were symbols of God's covenant. It was God's sky-writing in vivid color. "I am with you, my beloved daughter," I sensed Him saying to me.

Creator-God had sent me a personalized symbol of His love just when I needed Him most. He had sent virtual post-cards from heaven, laden with messages of His assurance. I breathed easier. A text I had read earlier that week came to mind: "There is one ray of hope; his compassion never ends" (Lam. 3:21,22, TLB). I couldn't help smiling. I had seen more than one ray of hope.

The next day my cousins and their friends came to the hospital in droves. They encircled my mother and me with their love and prayers during the long hours as we sat waiting for news. Their circle reminded me of God's celestial note the day before.

While my dad recuperated, I browsed the web for an explanation of what I had seen on the plane. I learned that the circular phenomenon was the effect of refracted light on the moisture-laden atmosphere around the aircraft. Physicists and astronomers call it *aureole* or *glory*. I was enchanted. Mine eyes had seen the glory, and it was very good.

Prayer For Today

My Creator and Redeemer,
Mine eyes have seen Your glory,
And it brings such comfort
When I walk through these dark valleys.
Your unfailing love reaches
higher than the heavens.
I will sing your praises among the people—
Among my family and friends.
I will shout Your name among the nations.
Your truth reaches to the clouds.
You display them in loving color.
And it is very good.
Amen

A Matter Of Patience

Wait for the lord;
Be strong and let your heart take courage;
Wait for the Lord.
Psalm 27:14, NRSV.

I was terrified. Sitting in my ophthalmologist's chair as he did the yearly exam, I suddenly realized that I could not see out of my left eye—I could not even see the eye chart. A huge black spot was all that was visible to me. What had happened? When did all this happen? Why had I not recognized a difference in my vision during the year? A dozen questions flooded my frantic brain.

Scared, I tried to listen as the doctor made an appointment with a retina specialist right away. "But there's good news." His smile was consoling as he walked to my chair. "Laser surgery often takes care of problems like yours, though it is expensive."

Money seemed immaterial as I clung to that single glimmer of hope. Two days later I went to the specialist. He gave his diagnosis: macular degeneration and suggested the treatment. I had the operation the following week even though it meant that I could not be present at my son's doctoral graduation. For five days I had to stay out of the sunlight, but I gladly followed the doctor's orders.

On my next visit, there was no sign of improvement in my vision. Nor on the next. "Dear God," I prayed. "Is this your will for me?" Disappointment weighed heavily on my heart, but today's text gave me strength and courage. And I waited.

On the third visit my doctor could see signs of improvement. So could I. "You had the patience," he said happily. "Your sight will improve." I was overjoyed to find over the following weeks that he was correct. My eyesight was just as good as it had been the year before. My spiritual eyesight had become even clearer.

My late husband often quoted a line from King George VI's 1946 Christmas message. "Go out into the darkness and put your hand into the hand of God. That shall be to you better than light and safer than a known way."

When I went back to my ophthalmologist for a check-up last year, he ran me through a battery of tests. Then he called to his nurse, "Come see a miracle." I could not keep from smiling.

I had been in darkness in those terror-filled weeks. Now I can do nothing but praise God for pointing me to a place filled with his Son-light. What a miracle-working God we serve!

Carol J. Greene

Prayer For Today

Thank You, dear Lord.
You helped me
Shun the perilous darkness of doubt.
Your promises are true.
You helped me learn to
Put my hand in Yours.
You taught me patience.
You brought me courage.
You gave me the desire of my heart.
I will wait on You
In total trust.
Amen

The Blessings Of A Frozen Shoulder

I waited patiently for the Lord;
And he inclined unto me,
And heard my cry.
Psalm 40:1, KJV.

A few years ago, I developed a frozen right shoulder. I am right-handed and the range of motion in that arm was severely restricting. Fortunately, I could still write and function at the computer, but zipping up my skirts or reaching to top shelves was awkward. The pain was becoming more intense with each passing day. I needed help. Four weeks of physical therapy brought no reprieve. I prayed for relief. So did my parents and scores of family members and friends scattered across the globe. Nothing seemed to happen.

Eventually my physician suggested that I see another doctor in a neighboring state even though my medical insurance would not cover that cost. She told me that she had worked with the therapist during her residency and was amazed at the progress of the patients in his care.

Traveling the 40 miles to his clinic at sunrise twice a week, I spent the time communing with my Father. One golden morning I wondered aloud if my lack of progress correlated with my wavering faith. I got no immediate answer then. But during the agonizing process of that morning's therapy, I was stunned at the doctor's suggestion.

"During the half hour it takes to come down here for therapy, why don't you spend the time praying or saying the shepherd's psalm. That should relax you. It definitely will make the session easier on us both."

I knew that my not-so-muffled screams as he tried to reeducate my muscles distressed him but I could not resist asking why he thought he could risk talking about religious matters to me. "I don't usually," he admitted. "But I saw the name of your university on your t-shirt. I know what that university stands for and I can see that you represent its mission. You never swear. You rarely complain and by the time the session is over, your ubiquitous smile is back in place." His smile mirrored my own.

I telegraphed a silent message to my Heavenly Physician. "Thank You for providing the context for wordless witness even if it brings pain for a moment."

Prayer For Today

Thank You, Physician Shepherd,
For giving me the faith to accept Your "Not yet"
As I move forward in my spiritual journey.
Thank You for reminding me that
You have a plan for me—
One that is bigger, better and
brighter than my own.
Thank You for hearing my wordless cries.
Thank You for Your reminder that
You always answer.
Thank You for helping me to become
Your silent witness.
Thank You for walking this dark valley with me
And bringing me Light.
I will wait on You
In total trust.
Always.
Amen

I Will Not Be Afraid For You Are Close Beside Me

There's A Man In My Room

For he orders his angels to protect you
wherever you go.
The Lord says, "I will rescue those who love me.
I will protect those who trust in me."
Psalm 91:11 & 14, NLT.

I once conducted a women's seminar in a delightfully remote region in Wisconsin. The wonderfully efficient person who called to give me directions to the meeting place confirmed that it was about six hours away from where I lived in Michigan. Since I could not start traveling until mid-afternoon, she promised to prepare the receptionist at the lodge for my 10:30 p.m. arrival. All I had to do was pick up the key when I got there.

Keeping an occasional eye on the map on the appointed day, I drove through the lush green lowlands of the three states that brought me to my destination. The summer breeze was a balmy reminder of God's love as I bypassed the metropolises of Chicago and Milwaukee. The highways were relatively unclogged.

Arriving at the lodge shortly after the stars came out on the darkening sky, I picked up the key to Room 9. Walking down the outdoor corridor, I marveled at the homey touch of the motel. I could see inviting lamplight through the curtained windows of my new room. At the door, I could hear that even the TV was on.

I inserted the key into the lock. Cold shock waves rushed through my body. A man, draped in bedcovers, emerged from the bed. My bed! My mouth fell open. Words lay unspoken in my too-dry throat. I could neither fight nor flee from the shadowed room. Moments dragged by on leaden feet. Then I heard a dry chuckle. "Glenda-mae, what are you doing in my room?"

"Praise the Lord," I exhaled. "I know this man." It was only then that I realized that I had been holding my breath. The 'intruder' was my sister-in-law's uncle. He too had come to make a presentation at the conference. The receptionist had inadvertently given him a key that opened all the doors of the lodge. Since he had stayed in Room 9 on previous visits, he had assumed that his favorite room was again assigned to him.

Settling into Room 7 that night, I barricaded the door and knelt by the bed to count my blessings. I had been protected. The 'unexpected guest' in my room was part of my extended family. As I reached for my Bible, I paused at several promises until I found the favored one. "Do not fear, for I am with you." (Isaiah 43:5, NRSV). Gratitude enveloped me. Faith had answered the door to my fear. The Ever-Present Shepherd had rescued me. I was safe.

As an added bonus, the Master Speaker had given me a powerful opening for my 'How to handle stress' presentation the next day!

Prayer For Today

Your promises are true, Gentle Shepherd.
I need never be afraid,
Because You show me the perfect way,

And walk beside me as I follow.
I need never be afraid, Gentle Shepherd,
Because You watch over me.
I need never be afraid, Gentle Shepherd,
Because You give me faith to answer
the door to my fear.
I praise You, Holy God.
Always and forever.
Amen

A Reason To Praise

The Lord is my strength and my shield;
My hearts in Him, and I am helped;
Therefore my heart exults,
And with my song I shall thank Him.
Psalm 28:7, NASV.

It was a foggy, gray evening. My dad was driving my mom and my brother to a meeting at our church. Suddenly a van went through a stop sign the driver did not see. It crashed into our family's car just inches from where my brother was sitting. The dashboard fell in. Glass was everywhere. Our car spun all over the road and eventually landed 40 meters (130 feet) from where the collision occurred. The car was a wreck. Blood dripped from my father's face. My mom was squished by the seat belt she was wearing. My brother was really scared. Everyone was badly shaken.

When my mom arrived at the church where I was helping with the children's program, she told me about the accident. I could not hold back the tears. My friends put their arms around me to comfort me. Then our minister took us into another room to pray together. I wanted to ask why God had not sent His angels. Then I realized that He had. He had sent me a double portion of heavenly and earthly angels.

I have always loved my family, but since the accident they are even more special (although I still can't seem to resist teasing my brother). My grandparents, aunts, uncles, and cousins, who called to praise God for sparing us, are my family too. The people at my church are also part of my family. Even my own personal guardian angel (I like to call him Luigi) is part of my heavenly family. It makes me feel so special to have such a wonderful family.

I Will Not Be Afraid For You Are Close Beside Me

Last Christmas, I got a card from a great-aunt. It seems to say exactly how I feel. It reads:

Praise the Lord 'cause we're healthy!
Praise the Lord 'cause we're here.
Say a prayer of thanksgiving,
And then say one again!
Praise the Lord for His blessings.
Hallelujah! Amen.

Christine A. Greene
[Christine Greene was 12 years old when she wrote this personal account of her family's accident.]

Prayer For Today

Thank you, Shepherd Savior,
Your promises are true.
You stay close beside me.
I praise You, Shepherd Guardian,
For the angels You send to comfort us.
I love You, Shepherd Provider,
For the family and friends You give me.
Shepherd Savior, I will not be afraid
Because You are close beside me.
My heart trusts in You,
And I am helped.
I exalt You, Shepherd Redeemer.
I praise You for Your love and protection.
Amen

The Secret Visitor

The Lord himself watches over you!
The Lord stands beside you as your protective shade.
Psalm 121:5, NLT.

On the way to work one morning, I noticed that my left indicator light was not working properly. The light on the dashboard wouldn't blink when I tried to use it; it simply glowed. Pulling into the nearest service station, I asked the manager if he had time to fix it immediately. I thought that all he needed to do was put in a new bulb or replace a fuse.

"No problem," he said, smiling. "It'll only take a minute."

He returned some ten minutes later with a 12-inch ball of fuzz in his hands. "We'll have to make an appointment for tomorrow. This is your problem." Seeing my bewilderment, he went on. "I think you have a mouse using the insulation under your hood to make a nest. She's starting to chew on the wiring as well. The lights on the outside do not work either."

Goose bumps dotted my flesh. The thought of what would happen if I had been driving down the highway and suddenly felt a furry rodent climb up my leg boggled my mind. Accurately diagnosing the cause of my distress, he soothed. "Don't worry." His voice was gentle. "It's under the hood. It can't creep inside. We'll take care of your car first thing tomorrow."

Going back to my Jeep, gleaming in freshly waxed black and gold splendor, I wondered at the startling turn of events. No one would ever know what was under the hood. I couldn't wait to regale my friends with the latest development. “There are mice all around,” a colleague said, reminding me that we lived in rural Michigan. “Didn’t you notice calling cards in the garage?” he asked. I hadn’t.

“It’s what’s inside that counts,” our preacher told us one day. It didn’t matter that on the outside my car looked the picture of perfection. It’s what happens when we are put to the test that matters. As was the case with my indicator lights, the real test is in how we respond when we are called to labor.

Prayer For Today

Precious Savior, I will not be afraid
For You keep a close watch over me.
Put me to the test, dear Lord.
Though the way is difficult,
The journey hard,
When You stand beside me,
I can show the world that
It’s what’s inside that counts.
With Your help,
The victory is won
Because You watch over me.
I need never be afraid, Gentle Shepherd.
You are here.
Amen

Your Rod and Staff Protect and Comfort Me

Angel In A Pickuup Truck

For he orders his angels to protect you
wherever you go.
They will hold you up with their hands
To keep you from striking your foot on a stone.
Psalm 91:11, 12, NLT.

On my way to work one beautiful spring morning, I drove by country roads lined with blossoming dogwoods. Stopping to yield to oncoming cross traffic, I noticed a blue pickup truck inching up behind me. I thought nothing of it until I began to track how closely it followed me for the next seven miles. I braked; it slowed down. I sped up; it accelerated. Puzzled, I glanced at the rearview mirror. I did not recognize the driver. His tousled blond curls were as unfamiliar as his vehicle. Clearly I was being followed.

I turned right; so did he. I checked my rearview mirror again. He was neither a colleague nor a student that I could recognize.

Turning onto the university campus, I noticed that he was still right behind me. When I drove into the safety of my parking space, he pulled up behind me. I got out of my car. He got out of his. Curious, I waited for him to join me on the relative safety of the crowd-filled sidewalk.

"Ma'am," his midwestern drawl was obvious. "Your brake lights aren't working. I almost slammed into you a few miles down the road. I had to follow you all the way here to make sure you arrived safely."

Without waiting for my stammered words of gratitude, he climbed back into his truck and drove off. I never saw him again.

I may never know who that man was, but there is one thing I do know. He was an angel in working clothes—a God-sent reminder of the Shepherd's unflagging protection and care.

God taught me a lesson that day. Angels—our rods and staffs—come in different sizes. There is no such thing as the perfect model. That my good Samaritan did not look like my picture of an angel was irrelevant. He had simply answered a call to service. My angel needed to be neither articulate nor well dressed. Wrapping his words in layered tissues of immaculate or long-winded politeness was unnecessary. What I needed, unknown to me, was safety. My Father had sent that young man to provide exactly that.

Prayer For Today

Thank You, loving Lord,
For sending angels
I may never realize I need.
Thank You for delivering me
from my own carelessness.
Thank You for the assurance that
You know where we are and what we need.
You are indeed my refuge and strength.
I need never be afraid,
You are always with me.
Amen

The Lilac Comforter

What I want from you is your true thanks;
I want your promises fulfilled. Psalm 50:14, TLB.

My husband and I went to Europe about 30 years ago to attend a church convention in Austria. During our travel, we visited several countries. In England we stopped to visit friends and explore the countryside. Sight-seeing in London one day, we paused at a large flea market to do some shopping. I bought a beautiful lilac comforter I was sure my daughter would like. Because I was so sure that she would enjoy it, it didn't matter that the package was extremely cumbersome, or that our trip was not yet over. Nor did it matter that I would have to hand carry her gift from train station to train station until we began our return flight at Heathrow International Airport.

Two weeks later we deplaned in Toronto, laden with souvenirs and gifts, including the lilac comforter. Eagerly we distributed the presents we had bought along the way. Everyone was appreciative. Or so it seemed. I noticed, however, that my daughter did not appear as excited as I had expected. She said all the right words, but something was missing. When I visited her home, the comforter was never on her bed. Like Mary, the mother of Christ, I pondered those things in my heart.

Then a couple years ago, during one of her weekly calls, my daughter bemoaned the cold temperatures—a herald of the impending wintry blasts. "Mom," she told me. "I could never make it through these frigid nights without that comforter you gave me years ago." The long-awaited words of appreciation thrilled my ears. "At last," I thought to myself. "It took 25 years, but she has finally realized the value and warmth of my gift."

But during my early-morning walk the next day, I realized that I had not really shown appreciation for the priceless gift I had been given almost 2000 years ago. I had been even more delinquent than my daughter. I realized anew that my Heavenly Father has waited—and continues to wait—for me to show my appreciation in actions. Words are not enough.

Carol J. Greene

Prayer For Today

Father, let me not wait a second longer
To thank You,
To show You by the way I live
How much I appreciate the gift of
Your redeeming love.
And, Father, please accept the words of
Heart-felt appreciation that I offer today.

Your blessings are uncountable.
Your mercy is unstoppable.
I can but say again,
Thank You, majestic Lord.
Thank You.

Airport Samaritans

Now let your unfailing love comfort me,
Just as you promised me, your servant.
Surround me with your tender mercies so I may live.
Psalm 119:76, 77, NLT.

It was a muggy summer afternoon as Patricia, Denise and I disembarked in Chicago. We had spent five wonderful days at a conference in New Orleans. Now we desperately needed to make the final connection to the small airport close to home. Our previous flight had been delayed for more than two hours, but the steward suggested that if we hurried, we might make that last connection. We opted for speed. We had to make that last flight. We could not miss the special program at our church that evening.

Rushing to the gate, we were appalled to hear, "I'm sorry. The plane just took off. We could not wait. There is a thunderstorm threatening in the area. We have no later flights. But there is another airline that goes to your airport," the agent focused on our crestfallen faces. "They may have space on their next flight."

Intent on getting to my destination, I ignored the crowd of distraught people milling around, and raced toward the other terminal. Then I noticed something. Denise and Pat were not with me. I knew I could not leave without them. Scanning the crowd for my friends, I spotted them at the desk talking to a bedraggled teenager. Resigned, I retraced my steps. They had been comforting the young mother and her baby son, crawling fretfully on the dirty floor. Reaching the group, I heard part of the tearful tale. The young woman had never flown before and did not know how to handle this crisis. Her mother would be waiting pointlessly at the airport. Her boyfriend's phone was disconnected. She had very little money. Fatigue seemed to seep through her pores.

Without a moment's hesitation, Patricia came to the rescue. "We're going to find a way to that airport, be it by plane, bus, or car. And you can come with us."

The sun came out in that woman's eyes. She was now among protecting friends. Her problems were solved. Leaving the baby with us, she went to freshen up.

Patricia picked up the precious bundle and began to sing to him. It didn't matter that the baby's diaper needed changing, or that his sojourn on the well-trodden floor had left him grimy. As she sang, he smiled, and our hearts melted.

When the young mother returned, we gathered up her paraphernalia—baby carriage, car seat, diaper bag and tote bags—and trudged through miles of airport corridors to our new destination.

Following behind the tired but goal-directed little group, I could not help but marvel at the turn of events. Pharisee-like, I had been rushing to a religious service, while my friends paused to live that religion—to touch, reach out and help their neighbor.

I don't know if the young woman still remembers my friends' act of intentional kindness. I suspect she does. What I do know is that God had used them as ministering shepherds. They were His rod and staff.

Prayer For Today

You've done it again, dear Lord.
You've shown me that in comforting,
We find comfort and strength.
Amen

You Prepare a Feast For Me

A Ziplock Bag Of Cheerios

They ate the food of angels.
God gave them all they could hold.
Psalm 78:25, NLT.

The enormous moving van had just pulled out of my driveway that summer afternoon. Almost immediately my little golden-haired neighbor came dashing across the lawn. "Goodbye, Glenda-mae." She mouthed the words softly, trying not to cry. "This is for you." Reaching behind her, she pulled out all the heavy artillery of her four-year-old heart—a Ziploc bag of cheerios.

Trying to hide my own tears, I put her token of love in my purse for safekeeping. That precious gift meant very little to my friends who knew nothing about our three year-old ritual. But both her mother and I understood it and were moved.

When Lilly and her parents moved into the house next door, she was barely a year old. Her parents would bring her to visit at least once a week. She was a golden-eyed charmer. Sometimes she would even let me hold her while I read to her. Sometimes she would read to me. Her chuckles were my delight.

Early one morning her mother called in a panic. "I'm still on duty here at the hospital, and my husband has to leave for work right away. Can you take care of Lilly for me till I get home? It shouldn't take more than an hour or so."

Minutes later, the father gently laid his sleeping baby on my still-unmade bed and sped off to his assignment. I worried that the little girl would wake up screaming when she found herself in vaguely unfamiliar surroundings, but she simply smiled when the morning sun kissed her awake. Lifting her out of bed, we said our prayers, washed and went in search of breakfast. She didn't seem to want the orange juice, banana or yogurt I offered. I opened another cupboard. Her eyes lit up when she saw the box of cheerios.

"Bowl," she ordered. I brought a plastic one. "Spoon." Her directions were minimal. "Milk," was her final request. And so our weekly ritual was started.

Crunching on Lilly's cheerios on my flight to my new home the next day, I thought about a line C. S. Lewis once penned. "Pure and spontaneous pleasures are like patches of God-light in the woods of our experience." I knew I had experienced His light through Lilly that afternoon. For a second I imagined what the children of Israel must have experienced when they first tasted manna. Today's text underlines that experience through David's eyes—they tasted food for angels!

Prayer For Today

What can I do but thank You, gracious God,
For showing me through
a four-year-old angel's gift,
The blessings of giving that bring the most joy?

What can I do but gather the manna
You spread in my way each day?

What can I do but praise You
For those incredible moments of pure and
spontaneous pleasure!

What can I do but listen for Your voice
When I cry to You for help?

What can I do but dine in sumptuous pleasure
At the table You have prepared for me?
Amen

Dora's Dilemma

How sweet are your words to my taste,
Sweeter than honey to my mouth.
Psalm 119:103, NRSV.

"I came to fulfill a promise to you, Doc," Dora sailed into my office to announce. My raised eyebrows begged for clarification. "You said to remind you to invite a group of us for lunch sometime this semester. Now, when's the date?"

I grinned. The young graduate student's patience was eclipsed only by her brilliant smile. "I'm not into cooking at the moment," I explained "Right now juicing is the thing! I've uncovered a wonderful recipe for an extraordinary juice—carrots, celery, apples, kale, garlic—"

Her upstretched hands stayed my list before I could invite her to sample a glass. "Oh, please," she implored. "My sister went on that bandwagon last month." Her Haitian-American accent seemed more obvious in her distress. "She bought this book and set to work at the juicer. My mother and I could hardly wait to taste the juice of her labor. But when we took the first sip, we almost died." Her wry smile acknowledged the hyperbole.

"What happened?" I had to ask.

"We don't really know. She followed the directions exactly. I checked." She listed the ingredients of the now infamous juice, her hand motions shaping each word as she pronounced it.

It was my turn to interrupt. "Tell me what a clove of garlic is," I asked, not understanding the dome-shaped movement of her elegant fingers when she mentioned the savory herb. Laughter exploded though the office suite when she understood her sister's gaffe. She had used a large bulb of garlic instead of a tiny clove!

"Somebody should have told us," she exclaimed. "In our house we rarely use a recipe book, so we never needed to know the English meaning of 'clove.' Somebody should have told us."

Sometimes it is what we know that is critical. Always, it is Who we know that makes the difference—a difference between the sweet and the bitter; between life and death. Our gentle Shepherd Savior is more gracious than our taste buds. When we recoil in distress or disgust at the taste of calamity, He gives us His word—a taste of His goodness—to save us. "As for God, his way is perfect, and the word of the Lord is tried" (Ps. 18:30). God's word brings such honey to our souls.

Prayer For Today

Dear Savior,
Your long-suffering goodness
Knows no bounds.
Thank You for loving us.
Your promises have always been true.
You have granted us such sweetness,
And in exchange,
We have given you the bitterness
Of our arrogantly sinful ways.
Lead us, Gentle Shepherd,
Back to Your Word.
And may the words of our mouths,
And the sweet meditations of our hearts
Always be acceptable to You.
Amen

Split Pea Soup From My Heart

O Lord, what a variety of things you have made!
When you supply it, they gather it.
You open your hand to feed them,
And they are satisfied.
Psalm 104:24 & 28, NLT.

She is the epitome of a successful independent woman, this friend of mine. She is articulate, resourceful, multilingual, poised and beautiful. When she told me she was having outpatient surgery the following week, we immediately prayed for God's healing power to attend her. For the rest of the week, I prayed for her each morning, and twice on the day of the operation. But that was it. What more could I do?

She called me from the recovery room that afternoon. "Praise God," she almost shouted. "I'm alive." I had no idea that she had struggled with that fear. Then she asked, "How long will it take to make me a pot of your split pea soup?"

Grateful that she needed something I could do, I hurried through the motions of making her supper. It was only a pot of soup—split peas, carrots, sweet potatoes, onions, blended with my signature seasonings and simmered on the stove.

I brought it to her later that evening, and sat with her as she savored it slowly. "Mmhh," she murmured through her bandages as she returned the bowl. "Thank you for sharing your gift with me." It took me a while to understand what she meant. She had tasted God's blessing in the soup.

This dish now represents more than mere sustenance. Often it means the warmth of fellowship for starving friends on chilly evenings; at other times we use it instead of a get-well card for recuperating shut-ins.

I am no gourmet chef, but this pot is now special. Not just because of its flavor or texture, but because of what it has come to symbolize to us: a simple God-blessed gift from the heart.

Prayer For Today

Loving Lord, we are satisfied!
Thank You, gracious Redeemer, for showing us
That there are traces of You
In the simplest things.

Thank You for opening our eyes
To the fact that little becomes much
When Your blessing is there.

Thank You for using us to help others
Taste Your goodness.
Amen

In the Presence of My Enemies

Inside Out

But in my distress, I cried out to the Lord.
Yes, I prayed to my God for help. Psalm 18:6, NLT.

In my rather radical administrative salad days, I was scheduled to give a presentation to the Board of Trustees at the college where I worked. I was to push for a proposal that I was sure would improve the quality of student life. Hoping that the all-male board was observant, I flaunted my femininity. Instead of the usual dark pinstriped suit, I chose a well-made black crepe dress with long, flaring sleeves and a swirling skirt.

Knowing that I needed to keep the board members' attention riveted on the subject at hand, I did all the things required of a good communicator. During my discourse, I walked around the room, maintaining eye contact with each person and building up the interest that I sensed had been piqued.

As I concluded, two hands shot up—almost in unison. I acknowledged the man whose son I had taught some years before, and who, I was sure, supported my proposal.

"Excuse me," he began gently. "I don't mean to be out of line, but aren't you wearing your dress on the wrong side?"

Mortified, I looked down. He was right. The seams of the dress had been so carefully stitched that only very close scrutiny could reveal that the dress was indeed inside-out.

I have no idea how I got out of that situation, though several people later assured me that I managed to do so with a modicum of finesse. But I could not wait to get home to call my mother. Ruefully, I recounted my disastrous experience. Peals of laughter swept over the phone lines. I expected that.

Minutes later my mom managed to regain her composure. I steeled myself for the age-old maxim I knew was coming—"Pride goes before a fall." Instead she inquired simply, "Now what?" Floored for the second time that day, I pondered her question.

It took years to find an answer. When I came across a Terry McMillan quote, I knew I had found an almost- perfect rejoinder. "Can't nothing make your life work if you ain't the architect."

Calamities are stressful, but the way we perceive them and subsequently structure our lives is far more critical. That dress incident was rather insignificant in the grand scheme of things. It was neither soul-shattering nor life-threatening. I would get over it. In ten years, according to my former creative writing professor, it would even seem funny, and he was right! Now, like King David the psalmist, I have a new prayer to guide me. I will not let my haughty look or arrogance (Ps. 101:5) stand in the way of a walk with Him.

Prayer For Today

Architect of my life,
Thank You for being there for me.
You know so much about me—
My secret pride-filled sins and

the more blatant ones,
And still You stay close to me.
Thank you for pointing out my flaws
Even if the process is painful.
Thank you for giving me directions
Even when I don't seem to listen.
Thank you for bringing
Peace and laughter to this troubled soul of mine.
Please refashion my heart
So that even if I wear it inside out,
It will be just perfect.
Amen

Jerusalem, We Have A Problem

Sing a new song to the Lord; bless His name,
Each day proclaim the good news that He saves.
Publish His glorious deeds among the nations.
Tell everyone about the amazing things He does.
Psalm 96:2,3, NLT.

We were in church that morning, February 1, 2003, when our minister came to the pulpit. "At 8:59 this morning, the Columbia crashed somewhere above Texas. There were no survivors."

Our space coast congregation inhaled in a collective gasp. The orbiter had crashed just 16 minutes from landing. The astronauts had not even had a chance to say, "Houston, we have a problem." We experienced a gamut of emotions—shock, disbelief, anger and grief—in numbed silence. Then tears flowed down as prayers went up.

Scouring the papers for details, I found myself drawn to the diversity of five of the downed heroes. First I got a multi-forwarded e-mail from a woman who had attended a Steve Green concert, just 12 hours after the loss of Columbia. The Christian artist had been a friend of Captain Rick Husband, the unabashed Christian. He told the audience that the captain's wife had chosen Green's song, "God of Wonders" for one of the crew's wake-up calls. Husband had e-mailed Green, describing how overwhelming it was to view God's vast creation—His wonders—from space.

Then I learned about Michael Anderson, the mild-mannered African American payload commander whose self-assurance reflected his absolute confidence in his God. Next I read about the two 41-year-old women—one a flight surgeon, the other an aeronautical engineer—from different parts of the world. One was a Christian from Racine,

Wisconsin, the other a Hindu from Karnal, India. But both bonded through their zest for detail and their love of a science that uncovers the awesome universe.

Almost a week later, they held a memorial at the Kennedy Space Center in Florida. Rabbi Zvi Konikov described his quandary at Ilian Ramon's question. The Israeli astronaut wanted to observe the Sabbath of his people. "How does one mark the Sabbath in space, with every 90 minutes another sunset; every 10-and-a-half hours a Sabbath?" "Jerusalem, we have a problem," he quipped.

Ramon's answer to his own query was the epitome of depth. "No matter how fast we're going, no matter how important our work, we need to pause and think about why we're here on Earth."* In other words, we need to consider the *raison d'etre* of our existence—our mission, as it were.

Those seven astronauts knew they were taking a risk when they blasted off into space. Our Savior took an even greater risk. He created us with freedom of choice; and when we chose to creep into enemy territory, He risked His life to save us—fallen mankind. He too had a mission.

New Jerusalem, we don't have a problem. We have the solution. Faith in Christ's redeeming blood; a faith we will share with others. Whoever we are, wherever we are, all we have to do is call upon Him, and He will help us to proclaim the good news that Jesus saves. Then we can exhale.

*Florida Today, February 8, 2003. Special supplement.

Prayer For Today

Commander of my life,
Shepherd of my days,
I need you.
I know why You came to earth,

And I am grateful.
No matter how fast we're going,
No matter how important our work,
Help us pause to think about something
even more important—
The reason why we're here on Earth.
Please let me reflect Your glorious deeds.
And tell of Your saving wonders,
On Your terms.
Amen

He Spat On Me

Answer me when I call,
O God who declares me innocent.
Take away my distress,
Have mercy on me and hear my prayer.
Let the smile of your face shine on us, Lord.
Psalm 4:1, 6, NLT.

Our family reunion time was coming to an end. Soon we would have to separate, leave our parents' house in Florida and return to our own homes. "Let's go to Disney World one last time," my nephew begged. "Please." It was a reasonable request for a little boy who lived in Saskatchewan and probably could not return as often as the rest of us. Nine of us piled into cars and off we went.

We had a wonderful time. We explored the sights and sounds. We tasted new foods. We screamed as the roller coaster rides took us to the edge of terror. Just before we were about to leave, we decided on one last ride, even though the line for that attraction snaked lengthily on the paths.

Waiting for the queue to inch along, I succumbed to my nieces' pleas and went to purchase some unusual balloons from a nearby kiosk. Joining the family in line again, I heard a man's disgruntled mutter across from us. "Some people have to stand in line for hours." We stood in line for what seemed like ages, hardly moving more than a foot per minute. A man's cough from the floor above us caused me to look up involuntarily, but there was nothing unusual.

Finally we moved closer to the turnstile. And then I saw it. The glob of phlegm that lay splattered on the blue sports jacket ahead of me. The new jacket my sister-in-law was wearing! I was horrified. So was her husband. "It's fine," Verla assured us, hurriedly dabbing at the offending mark with disposable wipes.

But somehow when I was assured that all was well, unstoppable mirth bubbled up inside me. I looked to my brothers for help, but I could see that they were having the same problem. One was biting his lips in an attempt to strangle the impending guffaws. The other, swallowing his chuckles, had moved away from us. I bit my own lips. I turned away, but it was to no avail. I lost the battle and doubled over in mirth.

And then they saw them! The three globs of phlegm splashed on *my* jacket. It was too much! My brothers lost their battles with restraint, so did their wives, and their children. So did I. Uncontrollable merriment littered the park.

I don't remember if we took that last ride, but what I do remember is that when we came home and regaled everyone else with my tale of woe, nobody could keep a straight face. No one even tried.

A week later, my younger brother called me. He was still chuckling at his recollection of my distress. "Now," he asked, sobering up enough to appear professional. "What are you going to do about it?"

"Write about it, of course." I praised God for the psalmist David's example. "And whatever else it takes, I'll pray." Moving nearer to the phone, we thanked God for the knowledge of His closeness. I thanked Him for loving family. My brother thanked Him for unrestrained joy. And in our prayer, we realized the accuracy of the late Henri Nouwan's reflection. Praying is discovering yourself, your God and your neighbor.

Prayer For Today

Heavenly father, look down upon me,
Your sin-splattered child.
Cleanse me from all unrighteous,
Regardless of how dreadful the
method may need to be.
Bless our neighbors
Even when they despise us.

Thank You for humor—
The irrepressible bubble
that makes our souls glad.
Thank You for family—
The network in our lives.
Thank You for prayer—
That wonderful connection with You.
Thank You for praise—
The means of honoring You.

Nourish our souls with Your abiding love.
Let the smile of Your face shine upon us.
May all who praise Your name
Be filled with abundant joy.
Amen

You Welcome Me As a Guest, Anointing My Head With Oil

God's Agenda

For you, O Lord, have made me glad by your work;
At the works of your hands I sing for joy.
How great are your works, O Lord!
Your thoughts are very deep.
You have poured over me fresh oil. Psalm 92:4,5,10, NRSV.

About to fly back to Michigan one evening, I discovered that I had horrendous connections in Dallas and a five-hour layover in Chicago. I called the airlines. "Isn't there a better way?" I queried. "There is another flight," the ticket agent confirmed, "But that will give you only 20 minutes to make the Chicago connection, and it is at a different terminal. Federal regulations do not permit me to book you on that flight. If you can make it, there are seats available."

"Please, Lord," I prayed. "Help me make that connection."

But it was not His will. My plane was delayed at the Dallas terminal. When I finally arrived in Chicago, I reached for the layover agenda I had made. There were letters to write, bookstores to visit, magazines to read. My activities were interrupted, however, by a red headed toddler who seemed fascinated by the intricate designs on my cane. His mother rushed over to scoop the little fellow into her arms and apologize for the disturbance. Or so it seemed to me for she spoke very little English.

"It's OK," I soothed, for apologies like smiles are universally understood. That phrase must have been comforting for she left her son with me and returned to a heated debate with her husband. She returned minutes later with two crumpled dollar bills in her hand and tears in her eyes. "Is enough? Call Mama?"

I had no idea where her mother lived but was quite sure that her telephone conversation would require more money. I started to explain, but God gave me a better idea.

Removing my calling card from my wallet, I pantomimed our next plan of action. We walked to the phone booth together. After punching in my code, I handed her the receiver. She dialed some numbers. "Mama," she said as her tears began to flow again. I returned to my seat. She came back minutes later, beaming her thanks. Her husband's nod of gratitude reflected her smile.

I do not know the end of their story, but I understood that God wanted to review with me the exponential joy factor. He created a scene and watched me interact with the toddler and his mother. Then it was as if He stood back and waited for me to realize that to bring others joy would embed even more joy in my own heart.

Praise God for His agenda!

Prayer For Today

Creator God, You have made me glad
by Your works.
Thank You for horrible connections.
Thank You for reminding me that
no matter how grim the situation appears,
You have a plan for me.

You Welcome Me As a Guest, Anointing My Head With Oil

You are bigger than all my woes.
Your thoughts are very deep.
Help me remember that with
Your omniscient vision,
You see the bigger picture.

You poured over me the fresh oil
of a woman's smiles.
I know that blessings abound.
Your thoughts are indeed very deep.
You have better agenda.
Amen

She Made Up My Bed

I meditate on the work of your hands.
I stretch out my hands to you; my soul thirsts for you
like a parched land.
Psalm 143:5,6, NRSV.

In a flurry of preparation, I cooked, cleaned and did the laundry. My brother and his family were bringing our parents to welcome in the New Year with me. I was excited, but fatigue seeped through my pores. "Just for three minutes," I promised myself as I sank into my favorite armchair and closed my eyes. I had not yet made up the bed in the room where my brother's family would be staying. "There will be enough time," I assured myself.

The doorbell awakened me half an hour later. I rushed to the door to greet the family. As we sat around the supper table shortly afterwards, my youngest niece leaned over to whisper excitedly, "Auntie, I have something to show you."

"Not now, darling, I have some things I must do right now. But later, I promise." Huge tears welled up in the little girl's dark brown eyes, but she said nothing more. Clearly, there was something important I had to see, and I had to look at it right then. As the others started eating, I slipped out of my chair, telegraphed a message to my sister-in-law, and took Briana's outstretched hand.

Smiling, the child led me into a bedroom. The king-size bed was as perfectly made up as a five-year-old could manage it, comforter and all!

I was amazed. When the bed was new, making it by myself was a gargantuan task. Now a little girl had done it all by herself.

"I had to stand on the bed in my socks sometimes. But I did it, auntie. I did it." My niece was ecstatic.

It was my turn to choke back the tears. Where were my priorities? I had almost missed that special gift. And I had said I had something more important to do right then! How could I have said that, knowing the visit was brief?

God showers gifts upon us daily. He sends them and often we miss them. Sometimes, lost in the bustle of daily living, we do not even notice His handprints on each blessing we receive. Sometimes we put off looking for a later date.

Will we ever have enough time?

Prayer For Today

Forgive us, dear Lord,
We didn't recognize You.
You knocked,
And we promised ourselves to answer
When it was more convenient.
You welcomed us,
And we ignored Your magnanimous gesture.
You showered us with blessings,
And we did not see.
Help us understand that we
are Your honored guests.
Straighten our priorities.
Help us learn to trace Your hand in
everything we see,
In everything You do.
We are anointed with Your grace,
And we are blessed.
Amen

Gift Wrapping

He will judge your people in righteousness,
Your afflicted ones with justice.
He will defend the afflicted among the people
And save the children of the needy.
He will endure as long as the sun,
As long as the moon, though all generations.
Psalm 72: 2,4,5, NIV.

Two presents lay side by side under the tree one Christmas evening. Both were creatively wrapped. One was a square box wrapped and trimmed with old newspapers. The other was a narrow rectangle wrapped with 14 dollar bills.

"I'm prettier than you," the dollar-clad rectangle gushed.

And indeed she was. Three crisp dollar bills were arranged in a fan at the top of the box and sprinkled with glittering gold dust.

"It's what's inside that counts," Newsprint crackled from her perch by the popcorn ornaments.

"I bet I'm worth more," Dollar preened, counting the bills on her coat.

"Value is as value lasts." Newsprint was given to adapting maxims.

The gifts lay quiet for a time until Dollar could stand it no longer. "What's inside you?" she asked, trying to get a better view.

"A tiny cluster of beautiful orchids. It's a photograph my owner took on her honeymoon in Hawaii. She matted it with loving care, and put it in an antique copper frame. What about you?" Newsprint asked over Dollar's snickering.

"I have a gorgeous silver-plated spaghetti service. It was delivered to the store only this morning. None of that old stuff for me and my owner."

"Everyone has been young before, but not everyone learns from being old." That was all sage Newsprint would say. In time the wrappings were admired, the presents distributed and fawned over.

Two years later, the spaghetti server, now tarnished and dented, was sold at a garage sale for a dime. But twenty years later, the beautiful photograph still hangs on the bedroom wall of those two special lovers.

Newsprint was right. The gift is not in the wrapping. It's what's inside that counts. Our physical blemishes may frustrate us. They may even handicap our interaction with others. But they will not affect our relationship with our Redeemer. Thank God, He looks at our hearts and welcomes us into His presence.

Prayer For Today

Father, our physical blemishes may frustrate us.
Our handicaps may hamper our progress.
Remind us, Gentle Shepherd,
That Your grace is sufficient for us.
You defend us with justice.
You judge us with mercy.
You show us that it is
What's in our heart that counts.
You anoint us with the oil of Your Holy Spirit
Throughout all the generations,
As long as the Son endures.
And we praise You.
Amen

My Cup Overflows With Blessings

Stuffed Srawberries

O Lord, how manifold are your works!
When you open your hand,
They are filled with good things. Psalm 104:24,28, NRSV.

A colleague asked me to host a group of students in my home for vespers one evening. I swallowed hard, caught on the cusp of a personal dilemma. I wanted to entertain the young scholars but I knew I had no more than $7 of disposable cash.

"It'll be only about ten of them," my friend continued. I accepted willingly. It simply entailed providing light refreshments, and my cupboards were not exactly empty.

But I wanted the students to experience a very special welcome. Rummaging through my purse, I searched for money I might have overlooked. I discovered instead the check for last week's tithe that had been missing since that church service. I paused for a nanosecond. I would not use it. Nor would I use my credit card.

Driving along the country roads that afternoon, I spotted a roadside fruit stand where huge red strawberries were on sale. Moments later, with two baskets of the luscious berries in one hand, and $2 in the other, I walked triumphantly to the car. Stuffed strawberries, I decided, would be that Friday evening's specialty.

As I stuffed the berries with a delicately flavored cream filling, I used the time to commune with God. As the music floated from my stereo, I prayed for a blessing on our gathering—my guests and the program.

Just before the sun set, laughing students spilled from their cars. Clearly I was about to host more than 30 students. Could they all fit in my modest ranch house? Would I have enough food? I left the details of the programming to the Father and went to the door to welcome each guest warmly.

We had a lively songfest. Then the young adults broke up into small discussion groups to talk about God's love. They spread all through the house. Some prayed in the bedrooms, others knelt in the dining room, yet others moved to the kitchen. Some even bowed by the dryer in the laundry room. The walls of my house seemed to expand. I could feel God's blessing upon us.

After we formed a circle of prayer around the dining table, we sat down to eat. The food seemed to take on the dynamics of those five barley loaves some 2000 years ago. It was enough, and it was good.

But that ending was only the beginning. Three days later, I felt a gentle tap on my shoulder. "Your tire has gone flat," one of my Friday evening guests reported sadly. "But I have a free period right now. I'll help you change it."

As he put away the jack, he smiled. "I'm so glad I got to know you."

I was the happy one. It had finally occurred to me that although the strawberries with their creamy centers were to be focal point of that Friday's celebration, God had a different agenda. He intended to open my eyes to the blessings—both material and spiritual—that He had been stuffing into my life all along. And I will never have enough room to hold them all!

Prayer For Today

Giver of all good things,
Restorer of peace and safety,
I give you grateful thanks
For filling my heart
With wisdom and praise.

You have filled my cup of joy
So that it flows over the brim
And blesses others
With its richness.

Thank You for opening Your hand
With all its goodness to me.
Thank You for knowing me.
Thank You for allowing me
To get to know You
Better each day.
Amen

Soggy Bread

Those who sow in tears shall reap in joy.
He who continually goes forth weeping,
Bearing seed for sowing shall doubtless
Come again with rejoicing,
Bringing his sheaves with him.
Psalm 126:5,6, NKJV.

We had opened the Bibles of our minds to Ecclesiastes 11: 1. We all knew that text by heart. "Cast they bread upon the waters for thou shall find it after many days." I remember a question that could have been sophisticated. "And what shall you find? Soggy, waterlogged bread?"

Our responses ran from amused chuckles to pensive deliberation. Then there was silence. Unable to leave the question untouched, I gave an answer only the Spirit could have shaped. "Of course not! That bread is waterproof. It has special preservatives." It took years for me to see how accurate that answer was.

My parents had developed a charming tradition for family birthdays. Tucked in our birthday cards were dollar bills representing each year of our lives. It did not matter whether the honored person was 3, 43, or 73.

Just before my birthday, my mother inquired, "Would you prefer to have a subscription to that religious journal instead?" Recalling the pleasant hours I had spent in her study, reading the cutting-edge articles, I promptly agreed.

When the journals arrived, I spent every weekend rifling through each issue, eagerly perusing the pages, then stacking them into piles. Although the piles began to take over my small study, I couldn't bear to throw them out.

Then I got an idea. Saving a special few, I gave the rest to my friends—unknowingly casting out the proverbial bread. They seemed delighted.

Eventually one woman asked for all the issues I didn't want to keep. I learned later that after reading them herself, she would read them again to her husband when they took long road trips. Eventually she gave them to her daughter who was in law school several states away. Her daughter shared them with others.

I found the bread when I saw the glow on my friend's face as she told story after story of renewed or newfound faith. I learned then that the bread does indeed have special preservatives. What's more, the water on which it is cast develops in us, the casters, the pass-it-on philosophy of a generous mind-set.

Prayer For Today

Thank You, Redeemer God,
For that great mandate.
I will cast my bread upon the waters.
Thank You for faith-filled eyes
That help us recognize
The gloriously enhanced bread
When it comes back to bless us.
Amen

Cracked China

Better is the little of the righteous
Than the abundance of many wicked.
Psalm 37:16, NASV.

Walking through the streets of downtown Toronto, I saw an elegant set of china in an unusual contemporary styling. I had to go into the store for a closer look. "It's a luncheon set, service for eight," the proprietor informed me with his aristocratic accent.

I was enchanted. The price was right. I planned how I would use the plates for special luncheons. An elegant setting would mask the fact the truth: I cannot cook.

On that first weekend, exclamations of aesthetic approval prefaced the collegiate chatter. But later, when a helpful young man, almost dropped a plate, I began to reconsider my decision. "Maybe I should use these for more mature guests," I mused. So I packed the dishes back in their boxes. Five years later I made a disheartening discovery. Two of the plates were cracked.

"The dishes were made to be used, madam," the proprietor told me when I called to complain. "If you won't use them constantly, at least soak them regularly."

That evening as I slid the fragile crockery into the soapy water, I paused, aghast at my past action. I had been storing up earthly treasures, thinking them too precious for use by the unsophisticated. My china had become more important than those brilliant young scholars who were willing to risk indigestion to share their afternoons with me.

I began to understand what Jesus meant when He lamented about how hard it was for the rich to enter the kingdom (Mark 10:25). I wasn't even rich. I simply owned 38 pieces of fine china, yet I was allowing them to block my path to the kingdom.

Distressed, I began to wonder. "Have I been hoarding more than china? Did I have other talents packed away?" Almost immediately, unused talents came to mind. Duly chastened, I opened my Bible to a red-lined verse. "Do not store up for yourselves treasures on earth, where moth and rust consume and where thieves break through and steal; but store up for yourselves treasures in heaven" (Matt. 6:19, 20, NRSV). I vowed to adjust my lifestyle.

As the china came out of hiding, so did my talents, including some I had not even realized I possessed. And I'm loving every moment of the spontaneous acts of sharing. Now that is heaven-stored treasure!

Prayer For Today

Lord, You've poured out such
abundant blessings on me
That I'm drinking from the saucer
Because my cup has spilled over.

Thank You for the earthly cracks and the rust
That remind us of the value of
Your heavenly kingdom.

You taught me how to store up
treasures in heaven.
I will learn from Your example.
Help me to share my blessings.
Because of Your goodness,
My cup has spilled over.
Amen

Your Goodness and Unfailing Love Pursue Me

Love Notes

I love you, O Lord, my strength.
The Lord is my rock, my fortress,
And my deliverer;
In whom I take refuge. Psalm 18:1,2, NIV.

When she was five, my granddaughter came for Thanksgiving dinner. As the rest of us got busy with the last-minute preparations for the meal, she retired to my study. It was only after she left with her family that evening that I noticed something heartwarmingly special.

Little Briana had printed a three-word line on several pages of a post-it note pad. Then she pasted the notes on walls over the house. The words, "I love you," declared her affection everywhere. I saw it on my desk. I noticed it on my refrigerator. I glimpsed it in her scribbles by the telephones. I was pursued by her love.

Her words reminded me that notes of God's love are written everywhere in our world. We see it in the beauty of creation—from the pristine beauty of a golden sunrise to the awesome glory of a coral lavender sunset. We feel it in the gentle breezes. I sense it in the tangy aroma of the orange blossoms. We taste it in the crispy crunch of a just-pulled carrot. I hear it in the gentle cooing of the doves each evening.

Briana's notes also reminded of the tiny box of scripture message cards that a friend had given me. Every word assures me of God's love and His promise to care, protect and guide us if we would but let Him.

"Everything speaks and acts of the Creator. Clouds and sunshine, dew and rain, wind and storm, all are under the supervision of God and yield implicit obedience to his command" (Ellen G. White, *Christ's Object Lessons* [Silver Spring, MD: Better Living publications, 1990], p. 81).

In Song of Solomon 2:4, King Solomon reminded us some four millennia ago, "His banner over me is love." The same phenomenon applies today. We have to keep our eyes and minds open to His notes of love. Letting His banner go unfurled, unread, or unheeded is unthinkable.

Carol J. Greene

Prayer For Today

Lord, Your goodness and
unfailing love pursue me.
Help me show my gratitude today
By befriending the unlovely and the lovely.
You did it, gentle Shepherd.
Show me how.
Amen

The Amazing D

For the Lord God is our light and protector.
He gives grace and glory.
No good thing will the Lord withhold from
those who do what is right.
Psalm 84:11, NLT.

It was my final year in college. My advisor did one last check of my transcript to ensure that all requisites for my graduation were accounted for. "There's still one thing missing," he told me. "It's the same thing that's been missing for the last two years." My heart sank as it had each time he had reminded me. "You still need one credit of physical education. You must register for it *this* quarter." His baritone underlined the timeframe as he handed me the class schedule.

My eye-hand coordination is virtually non-existent so I never excelled in sports. Way back then, an administrative accommodation for this deficiency was unheard of. Dismissing volleyball, tennis, and basketball, we paused at golf. Surely it was slow-paced enough for me to handle. Then I hit a roadblock. The rental equipment had already been spoken for, and I could not afford to purchase my own clubs.

"What about badminton?" My professor pulled his spectacles down to ask. "Surely you can do that. It's fairly straightforward. My daughters love it."

I signed up for the course. The first class went well as I learned the rules of the game. We went on the court for the second class. Things went well until I discovered that ducking the shuttlecock as it was volleyed over the net was unacceptable. I had to return it. "You can't close your eyes each time the birdie comes your way." My classmates were kind. Yet I still flinched each time I had to return the shuttle. I prayed about my problem, but it seemed to make no difference.

I came to dread Tuesdays—the day we were on the court. Valiantly, my instructor gave me tips to improve my game, but I still had problems. By the end of the term, it was clear that any chances for improvement were slim. I was not measuring up to the requirements of the game. My hopes for passing the class dimmed.

Three days before graduation, the final grades were published. Hesitantly, I walked across campus to scan the physical education roster. Slowly my eyes ran down the list. They stopped, in amazement, at my name. I had passed. With a D. But I had passed! Prayer does change things.

I got a new perspective on the grace the apostle Paul talks about. "For by grace you have been saved through faith, and that not of yourselves; it is the gift of God, not of works lest anyone should boast" (Eph. 2:8, 9, NKJV). We don't measure up, but God does.

A gift of grace is always something that is undeserved and unearned. It is God's gift to us. That's what's so amazing about the glorious gift of God's grace!

Prayer For Today

I don't measure up, Merciful Shepherd.
Your fleet-footed pursuit of this bumbling sinner
Mystifies me.
I will sing of Your goodness.
I will tell of Your amazing grace.
You are my defense in stress-filled moments.
You are my refuge in times of trouble.
You are my strength when I falter.
I will praise Your name
Always and forever.
Amen

Foiled

I will praise you, O Lord,
For you have rescued me.
You refused to let my enemies triumph over me.
Psalm 30:1, NLT.

"Has anyone experienced a miracle in her life recently?" A woman in our prayer circle asked. It was a good question. Several women shared very moving experiences. Personally, I could think of nothing more powerful than the amazing miracle of life. Fortunately we ran out of time before I could speak.

As we passed a service station a few days later, I saw an ancient white Fiat. Suddenly memories, four decades old, flooded my consciousness.

"Stop, my friend. Stop. That's my car!" I remember waking up to the midnight commotion of my father's urgent distress call. We lived, way back then, in rural Jamaica. "Stop, friend. Stop. That's my car." My father's pleas seemed incessant.

I slid out of my little girl's bed and hurried to the front room. I could see my father on the porch, his cupped hands encircling his mouth as he beseeched the car thieves. "My friend, please leave the car." I could hear my mom begging him to be quiet. I could feel my heart beating rapidly.

I could hear the car tires crunching on the gravel of our long driveway as the men pushed our little Fiat down the gentle incline. And suddenly there was silence. Then there was the sound of the emergency brakes being pulled up, car doors being slammed, and the rush of fleeing feet.

The policeman, who came in response to my mother's distress call, shook his head. "You are so lucky," he told us. The would-be burglars were a part of a drug heist. Three other cars had been stolen along this coastline. One had run out of gas a couple miles beyond us. Ours, apparently, was to be its substitute.

Later friends argued that our car had not been taken because my father called the criminals 'friends.' My mother knew differently. "What happened was a miracle," she told us in no uncertain terms that night. "It was God who foiled their plans."

I still remember going back to bed that night, comforted by that knowledge, and by the fact that I need not trudge those four long miles to school the next day. Years later I came across a powerful phrase an unknown writer once penned. "We cannot know how much we owe to Christ for the peace and protection we enjoy."

Prayer For Today

Thank You, majestic Maker of miracles,
For rescuing us,
For foiling the enemy's plans
every day of our lives
Even when we cannot see it.
Thank You for the peace and
protection we constantly enjoy.
Thank You for the privilege of calling You
Savior, Redeemer and Friend.

All the Days of My Life

Babyhood—Thank You

But giving thanks is a sacrifice that truly honors me.
If you keep to my path,
I will reveal to you the salvation of God.
Psalm 50:23, NLT.

Almost a decade ago, my brothers and their families joined me at our parents' Florida home for a special Christmas gathering. Delighting in the workings of the mind of children, I listened as my five-year old niece told her version of the story of the healing of 10 lepers as cited in Luke 17. We got involved in a deep discussion. "Were the lepers' sores related to leopard's spots?" she wanted to know.

I, on the other hand, wanted to figure out how well she understood the principles of subtraction, and how clearly she could apply the gratitude factor to that story. Using men from her cousin Jonathan's Lego set, I highlighted the agony of the 10 sick men and Jesus' healing compassion. Then, picking up a single piece, I told her that only one came back to say thanks. "Now, tell me," I said, my schoolteacher genes surfacing irresistibly as I arranged the pieces into two categories. "If only one came back, how many forgot to say thank you?"

She shot the right answer back almost immediately. Then she ended with a wistful query. "I would never forget to say thank you. How could they?"

Searching for an answer, I watched her baby sister start toward us. Picking up two additional men from her cousin's collection, the infant toddled over to our corner.

"Thank you," she lisped sweetly, placing the pieces beside the lone 'grateful' man. Then she marched back, determined to assist her cousin in his construction project.

Her older sister's quizzical expression reflected my surprise. Cousin Jonathan, who usually gets incensed when his set is disturbed, seemed untroubled as his eyes tracked the location of his choice pieces. Baby Briana too was unconcerned, or so it seemed to us. A thank you needed to be said. Nobody was doing it. So she did. Case closed. That she was rectifying a 2000-year omission was beyond her and therefore irrelevant. Gratitude is such a wonderful gift.

I wish I knew if that thank-you was a coincidence, or if that was really how the young child's mind worked. I shan't know until I get to heaven, but I am reminded that some coincidences are, in actuality, miracles in which God chooses to remain anonymous.

Prayer For Today

Thank You, dear Father
For all the wonderful miracles
You have performed—
All through the ages,
For all the gifts You have strewed along my path—
Tangible or intangible.
Giving You thanks is no sacrifice.
Giving You thanks is an extravagant honor.
I will keep to Your path.
Shine the light of Your presence on me,
All the days of my life,
And bring me peace.
Amen

Childhood—I Can Help

Behold, children are a heritage from the Lord,
The fruit of the womb is a reward.
Psalm 127:3, NKJV.

My husband and I were planning a trip from the North American far north to the far south. We could not make that decision, however, without finding out what it would mean for our two young daughters. So we took a fact-finding, are-we-going-to-like-this-place trip.

We took them to church. My baby daughter was charmed, for the first time giving me permission to leave her while I went to my own Bible study class. My husband went to the university he was considering. It met his requirements. We took the girls to visit their grandmothers. Delight on all sides. I checked out the job market. Definite possibilities. One final prerequisite: school for our older daughter. I prayed and hoped for a perfect match.

Takara was invited to spend a morning in a classroom. Bright-eyed with excitement, she took a seat. The other children listened to stories, did exercises, answered questions. My daughter said nothing. Only her eyes showed her involvement. Finally, a 6-year-old sitting close by could stand it no longer. He could tell, it seemed, that she wanted to share in the synergy of the classroom. To him, her silence could only mean one thing. Spanish, not English, must be her mother tongue. Politely, he tugged at the teacher's sleeve.

"Teacher, is it Spanish that she speaks?" he asked quietly. "*Permitale hablar. Yo ayudare a traduciv.* Let her talk. I can help. I'll translate."

I was moved by the young boy's thoughtfulness. His assumption about language was inaccurate—Takara just takes a while to check out the new environment, but when she feels comfortable, it's non-stop dialogue. However, that boy's mind was already on the way to understanding the principle of intercession. More important, he was practicing it.

Sensitive, Spirit-taught child wonder—a testimony to witness, this gracious youngster was prepared to curtail his own sharing to bring my daughter, a subdued stranger, into the circle of caring association.

Our investigative trip is now complete. The final decision affirmative, made easier because of one who cared enough to say, "I can help."

Now imagine this scene: a celestial circle with a throne, our Supreme Parent and ourselves. Consider the habitual sinner on the edge of the circle while our Elder Brother in the inner circle asks, "Father, let Me speak. I can translate. I've been there, and I speak the language."

Perhaps today I can invite someone into the circle of love.

Janet M. Greene

Prayer For Today

Caring Shepherd, You have walked these
dangerous roads before.
You know the way.
You understand the obstacles.
Thank you for substituting Yourself
At the throne of mercy.
You translated the words, Shepherd of love,
Your intercession sustains.
Your righteousness saves.
Thank you for bringing me into
Your circle of love
Amen

Adolescence—Even If I Sue?

That our sons may be as plants
grown up in their youth;
That our daughters may be as pillars,
Sculptured in palace style.
Happy are the people whose God is the Lord.
Psalm 144:12 &15, NRSV.

As we were driving down from the Rockies to a weekend getaway on a tiny island off the coast of British Columbia, Canada, my 13-year old nephew asked, "Auntie, will you pay my way through law school?" Delighted that he was giving serious consideration to post-secondary education, I responded. "Of course, darling."

"Even if I sued you for all the times you've mentioned my name in your teaching, your writing, or your preaching?" Benign mischief put a sparkle in his gray eyes.

I had to smother a smile. "Absolutely, my dearest."

"But why would you do that?" He seemed genuinely puzzled.

Before I could answer, his 15-year old sister looked up from an entry she was making in her blessings journal. "Unconditional love. That's why." Her response was matter-of-fact.

"You mean she'd really take her hard-earned money to pay my way through school, and then pay again when I sued her? That's a rip-off. A royal rip-off!" His whisper was incredulous.

His sister nodded. "She said she would, didn't she?" The muted conversation was clearly reserved for those in the back seat. "I think she's trying to be just like Jesus. He did something like that. He came to us with so much love, and we . . ."

I strained unsuccessfully to hear her words, but the wind from the open window blew them away. After we arrived on the island, my niece lingered in the sunshine, searching for colored starfish in the shallows. "We experienced a parable in the car this morning, didn't we?"

I started to answer before I realized that her question was rhetorical. Basking yet awhile in the summer sun, I meditated with my pen. "Creator God, You are truly amazing. You let us find You in most unexpected places. Thank You for letting me see Your grace in these youngsters—not quite grown. Thank You for allowing me to see Your sculpting process. Please, Lord, help them grow up to be fit for Your heavenly palace."

Prayer For Today

Ever-loving Redeemer,
You rescued me.
Thank You for helping me,
An earth-born sinner understand—
Even if only on a minuscule level—
The greatness of Your saving love
For all of us in this world.
And thank You for adolescents
Who remind me of how magnificent You are.
Please, Lord, help them grow up
As happy, healthy plants
Fit for Your heavenly palace.
Amen

Adulthood—The Wedding Of The Year

As the deer pants for streams of water,
So I long for You, O God,
I thirst for God, for the living God,
When can I come and stand before him.
Psalm 42:1,2, NLT.

We spent hours together, planning the wedding she had dreamed of since she was a little girl. The wedding was to be the talk of the town. She warned me that the bridal party was going to be huge, including a dozen of her girlfriends who would fly from cities all over the continent to celebrate this occasion with her. So would the attendant groomsmen.

Eagerly she showed me the pattern and the shimmering green material she had selected for her bridesmaids. She bubbled when she told me she had found a dressmaker who was willing to make all 12 dresses. The woman had promised that she would have them all waiting for the last-minute alterations when the bridesmaids flew into town on the weekend of the wedding.

It should have been simple. But a half hour before the ceremony was to begin, the phone in the church office rang. It was the maid of honor. "My dress isn't done," she said, tears dripping from her voice. "None of them are. Not a single one."

It was difficult for me to share the news with the bride and her mother, but once they got over the shock, they were resolute. "The wedding must go on." Fanning her perspiring mother, the bride brushed away her tears. "John and I will be married today. All I really need is one bridesmaid. Just one. Will you find one for me?"

Going up to the balcony, I looked over the crowd of guests. And then I found her—a high school friend of the bride, elegant in emerald green velvet. I reached her and started to explain the problem. "Don't worry," she soothed. "I'll stand in for Jackie."

It was a beautiful ceremony, though some wondered why there were 12 groomsmen and one solitary maid. I, in turn, wondered at the group of women who huddled together in apparent debate, climbed into a waiting car, and left before the service concluded.

What I learned later was that they had gone to do what author, Laurie Beth Jones (*Jesus, CEO* [New York: Hyperion, 1994], p. 127) describes as a WOWSE activity—realizing a vision With Or Without Someone Else. Each woman had tackled a dress—cutting, sewing, creatively putting the finishing touches on hems and sleeves with tape and even Velcro as the clock pointed to the reception hour.

Imagine the jubilation of the crowd when the entire bridal party, dressed in their wedding finery, entered the reception hall! Imagine the cooperative work that had been done. Imagine our celebration when, on that golden day, we see the Shepherd returning as a Groom prepared for His bride—that's us!

What are we doing to prepare for that glorious day?

Prayer For Today

Heavenly Bridegroom,
I long for your presence,
I thirst for Your love.
I am Yours
Today and always.
Help me put the finishing touches on my heart
In readiness for meeting You,
My one true love.
Amen

Middle age—Praise Song Of A Childless Mother

He gives the barren woman a home,
So that she becomes a happy mother.
Psalm 113:9. NLT.

"Would you read a poem in church for me?" a girlfriend called to ask a few days before Mother's Day. "I'm the presiding elder for our church service that day. I've written a poem celebrating mothers, but"—angst leaked almost imperceptibly from her voice—"but I can't read it in public. I don't want to cry." Mentally juggling my own schedule, I agreed.

Her poem was powerful, beautifully crafted and majestically inclusive. Mothers of all ages, stages, and ethnicities were represented. The church members and I were blessed.

Dashing to another church five miles down the road, I had time to wonder why I had never felt deprived by my childless state. "Is it that I'm too selfish, too focused on other things, Lord?" I asked my heavenly Passenger. His answer came in beautiful phases.

Arriving at the next church, I discovered that they were also celebrating mothers. Before the minister spoke, young people distributed carnations to all the congregants who were mothers. The pianist, a college student who always seemed to need to be in my office, brought me a ruffly pink flower. "You are my campus mom," he informed me with a gentle kiss. I had been deliberately included in that special celebration. At the end of the service, the choir director whispered. "Mentally, I dedicated the anthem to you, Mom." Again I felt part of the venerated group.

Picking up the mail that evening, I was delighted to find two Mother's Day cards from young women whom I had taught almost a decade earlier. One had scribbled a note. "You are indeed a mother in Israel." When my nieces called for what my sister termed "Other Mother's Day," my cup overflowed.

Almost a year later, as I waited in the doctor's office with an injured student, I was touched by his answer to the receptionist's quizzical look. "She wouldn't know my father's medical insurance number. She didn't birth me. She grew me. They do that at the university." Unwittingly the young man had explained why I had never felt deprived by my childless status. God had created a niche in which I had the blessed opportunity to function as a mother almost daily.

Prayer For Today

All-seeing God, You know all about us.
You know what we need,
And what we want.
You know how to give us happiness.
Give us Your love,
Give us Your wisdom.

Thank You for people to love,
And people who love us.
Thank you for niches into which we fit,
And people to explain our standing.
You give us Your love,
Please give us Your wisdom.

We will praise Your name forever.
Amen

Old age—Wisdom's Years

They will still bear fruit in old age,
They will stay fresh and green.
Psalm 92:14, NIV.

"How are you today?" I asked a neighbor who was pruning her roses.

"Old age isn't easy, you know my dear." The old woman stood up, slowly brushing clumps of dirt from her knees. Bewildered by the unusual response but enchanted by the singsong voice that betrayed her Caribbean heritage, I stopped to chat.

"Old age is like working for yourself. And the work is hard." Leaning on her gate she explained her metaphor. "First I struggle to get out of bed, and then I spend 10 minutes on my eyes, and another 10 on my teeth, and yet another 10 on my pained-up knees. And the list goes on and on."

At the crest of my own 70-year experience, I realized that I could relate to her woe. I wondered if my neighbor recognized how closely she had echoed Solomon's words in his poetic ode to old age. (Ecclesiastes 12). As I came upon verse 9 in a very contemporary translation of the Bible, I realized how reassuring Solomon's litany was to those of us who have passed middle age. "There is nothing more important for me than to . . . pass on to others what I have learned (*Clear Word* [Hagerstown, Md: Review and Herald Publishing, 1994], p. 759). Clearly, people who have attained the veneration of our state still have work to do.

When I read the lines below, attributed to a Middle Eastern mystic, I caught yet another glimpse of the developmental theme of living and praying.

"When I was young, I prayed, 'Lord, give me the energy to change the world.'

"When I approached middle age, I prayed, 'Lord, give me the grace to change those who come into contact with me—just my family and friends—and I shall be satisfied.'

"When I grew old, I prayed, 'Lord, give me the grace to change myself.'"

How tragic it is that we rarely become wise before we grow old. But praise God for the possibility of wisdom!

Carol J. Greene

Prayer For Today

Dear God, please give us wisdom and Your grace
To change ourselves first.
Then let us pass on our knowledge
to those around us.
Help us still to bring forth good fruit
in our old age.
Thank You for the assurance
That our talents will stay fresh and green,
Even though our bodies will not.
Amen

Death and Dying—This Is My Daughter

Weeping may endure for a night,
But joy comes in the morning.
Psalm 30:5, NKJV.

I walked down the hall of the ICU. I was going to visit my dad who was recuperating from another major surgical procedure. He smiled bravely when he saw me.

"Olivia, this is my daughter." My father was speaking to his charge nurse as clearly as the myriad tubes around his nose and mouth would allow. "She is . . ." And he went on to elaborate on what he regarded as my accomplishments.

About to halt his flow of kudos, the gentle movement of the nurse's capable hands stopped me. "Oh, how I wish my father would introduce me like that!" The voice that calmed my dad during his rough times was regretful. The almond-shaped eyes were moist.

I thought about that nurse's words when it became clear that my father's health was not going to improve. I thought about them with sadness when my father suggested, "Daughter, perhaps we can write out some of the things I want at the funeral." I thought about them with bittersweet emotions at his funeral. The standing-room-only affair was a foretaste of heaven. I know he would have enjoyed it because his family was there. So were his friends and cohorts. There was the music that he requested, and the laughter he had hoped for. Only the tears we could not avoid reminded us of the difference.

I thought about her words when we laid my beloved father to rest beneath a blanket of his favorite red roses. I thought about them as I clung to the blessed hope that I would see my dad on the golden resurrection morning. The apostle Peter reminds us of that vibrant hope. God the Father, he assured us, "through His abundant mercy has begotten us again to a living hope through the resurrection of Jesus Christ." (I Peter 1:3, NKJV)

I thought about that promise with joy as I longed for the day when I could finally lay my head on my Heavenly Father's shoulder. I thought about the privilege of hearing Him say, "This is my daughter. I am proud of her." And that made all the difference. I know I will see Him with my father that day. I must be ready.

There is peace in the valley. The resurrection is before us. "But God will redeem my soul from the power of the grave. For He shall receive me" (Psalm 49:15, NKJV). Now I can rejoice.

Prayer For Today

Father, thank You for walking through
the dark valley with me,
Without You my soul would have settled
In anguished silence.
With You, there is peace in the valley.
Thank you for triumphing over death.
Thank you for that You'll do it again
On that great resurrection day.
Thank you for that vibrant hope.
Help us to be ready to meet you.
Amen

I Will Live in the House of the Lord

That's Me!

The one thing I ask of the Lord—
the one thing I seek the most—
is to live in the house of the Lord
all the days of my life,
delighting in the Lord's perfections
and meditating in his Temple.
Psalm 27:4, NLT.

Just before the frenzy of the Christmas holidays began, some friends and their toddler son stopped by to visit. As we settled into the living room to catch up on the benchmarks of our professional journeys, I noticed that little Zachary was beginning to show signs of intense boredom. Taking him by the hand, I led him through the house, nonverbally granting him right of passage to any room he chose. Then I rejoined his parents.

Minutes went by before a beaming little boy came back to the front room and tugged at my hand. "Gina," he begged, calling me by a name he had decided should be mine. "Gina, come see!" He led me down the hall. His parents, unaware of the fact that most rooms in my house are virtually childproof, followed behind us. Trepidation hastened their steps.

Climbing up on the couch in the study, the little fellow pointed to three charcoal sketches by a famous Jamaican artist hanging on the wall. Singling out the drawing of an adorable little urchin in overalls, he turned to us. His bright eyes and broad smile mirrored the expression of the boy in portrait. "That's me," he informed us. "That's Zachary!" Relieved parents looked on in doting affirmation. He did indeed look like the child in the picture.

I put that precious incident in a spiritual frame a few days later. I realized that in two words—"That's me"—Zachary had captured the essence of being a Christian. As soon as we announce to the world that we are Christian, God measures us with His yardstick—His Son, Jesus Christ. And so will the world.

When people look at me, I want them to think, "Isn't she just like Jesus!" Our Heavenly Shepherd came to earth and endured excruciating agony to show us how to overcome the fruits of our foreparents' fall from grace. We have his God-breathed example to follow. We can be just like Jesus as we prepare to live with Him in His house forever.

Prayer For Today

Thank You, gentle Shepherd,
for that precious reminder.
Thank You for modeling the steps
that I must follow.
I want to be just like You.

You are my God, and I will praise You.
You are my God, and I will exalt You.
Nothing is impossible with You.
I want to be in Your kingdom.
Please, Lord, help me.
I want people to think
That I am just like You.
I want to know that I am just like You.
Amen

At The Sound Of His Voice

The voice of the Lord is powerful.
The voice of the Lord is full of majesty.
The Lord will bless his people with peace.
Psalm 29:4, 11, KJV.

He breezed into my office one summer morning and just stood there. I looked up expectantly. Still wordless, he stood in the doorway. I smiled. His eyes telegraphed a message to me, but I was clueless about either the message or his identity. His shoulders sagged almost imperceptibly, and then he spoke. "You mean I made a 200-mile detour just to see you, and you don't even know who I am?"

At the sound of his voice, the fog cleared. Springing up from my desk, I greeted him warmly. He had been one of my best friends more than a decade ago. We had worked together, counseling high school students. We had spent countless hours arguing about biblical perspectives, philosophies, current events, and dreams of ideal spouses. But we had not seen each other for years. The occasional phone call was the single link in our chain of communication. Without the signature timbre of his baritone, I would have passed him off as a total stranger.

Lunching with a girlfriend the next day, I regaled her with the story of our meeting. "I can't believe you," she exclaimed. "You've talked about him so often, and then you couldn't even recognize him when he came to visit." I gave several reasons why that might have happened. His dress sense had improved; he'd shed the beard I had never seen him without; he had lost more than 50 pounds. My girlfriend was not convinced. Neither was I.

Gradually a parallel between our friendship and my relationship with my heavenly Father became clear. When my friend and I worked together in the same location, we would notice even the subtlest changes in the other. But when we moved to separate sides of the country, we lost the daily communication on which our friendship was based. We lost the eyeball-to-eyeball and eardrum-to-eardrum dynamics on which our fellowship was grounded. Change eroded the stuff on which our relationship was based.

With our Shepherd Friend, however, nothing can separate us if we chose to keep Him in our hearts. He never changes. We can always recognize Him.

Praise God, our lines of communication need never be broken!

Prayer For Today

My Shepherd and my changeless Friend,
I know who You are.
Help me to recognize
Your voice everywhere—
In the gentle breeze,
Or the hesitant plea of a timid soul,
Or the call for extraordinary service.
May I never again leave You
Standing in the doorway of my heart.
May I never cause You to make further detours
To rescue me from this sin-sick world
Thank you that our lines of communication
Need never be broken again.
This sheep knows Your voice, O Master.
I will follow You
Wherever You lead.
Amen

Letter From Galilee

Happy are those who have
the God of Israel as their helper,
Whose hope is in the Lord their God.
He is the one who gives justice to the oppressed
And food to the hungry.
The Lord lifts the burdens of
those bent beneath their loads.
The Lord loves the righteous.
Psalm 146:5, 7, 8, 9, NLT.

Dear parents,

I've met the most marvelous man ever! I can guess the questions you will ask, so I'll answer them before you even speak them. I've met his mother—the sweetest, gentlest, most pure-minded woman I know. His father is no longer living. (There was some talk of illegitimacy but that is both untrue and irrelevant.)

I must warn you that one of His ancestors, Rahab, was a prostitute. But she changed. And what a change! You know the stories about the fantastic impact she made on those around her. Her faith saved our entire nation way back then.

Yes, Dad, he had a trade. Word is that he used to do the finest woodwork this side of Galilee. I say "used to" because he gave up carpentry almost three years ago. Now he journeys along the road, talking to people, teaching them, and healing some. He's wonderful at that. People travel for days to be with him, this itinerant, medical preacher.

You should hear him speak! I can hear the love of God in his voice. His words are so beautiful, so powerful, so life-changing that people even forget their growling stomachs. (One day I'll tell you about the miracle bread-and-fish lunches that he's shared with us.) Yesterday he said, "Don't worry. The sparrows never worry that they'll run out of seeds." I had never thought about it like that before. Just one line and everything comes into focus. Our God provides for us.

He has the most wonderful philosophy on happiness. This scroll is not long enough to tell you everything, and the messenger is waiting to take this letter to you. I will close with my favorite line. "You're blessed when you get your inside world—your mind and your heart—put right. Then you can see God in the outside world" (Matt. 5:8, Message). Because of Him, I can see that the earth is crammed with the light of God. I shall never be the same again.

Yes, I love him. But it's way beyond the love King Solomon wrote about. It's a love that I want to share with everyone around me. It is too special to keep to myself! And I want to live with Him forever.

Your loving, dedicated daughter,

Rebecca

Prayer For Today

Shepherd of my life,
I praise You.
Creator of my future,
I love You.
You are my focus setter,
You are my strength.
Marvelous are Your works,
Beautiful are Your words,
And that my soul knows quite well.
Thank You for preserving me.

Forever

Letter To My Shepherd Redeemer

There is a hole in my soul, dear Lord.
A heart-shaped hole.
A hole that only You can fill.
A hole that longs for a closer relationship with
You,
Only You.
I long for your presence,
I thirst for Your love.
I am Yours,
Today and always.

Thank You, dear Father
For all the wonderful miracles You have
performed—
All through the ages,
For all the gifts You have strewed along my path—
Tangible or intangible.
I have need of absolutely nothing.
I can trace Your hand
In everything I see.
Giving You thanks is an extravagant honor.

Shine the light of Your presence on me.
Guide me in the right direction
And bring me to the realization
That because You love me,

I will not be harmed
If I engrave Your instructions on my heart.

Thank You for walking through the long dark
valleys with me.
Without You my soul would have settled
In anguished silence.

You are my God, and I will praise You.
You are my God, and I will exalt You.
Help me put the finishing touches on my heart
In readiness for meeting You, my forever Friend.
Because of You, I am blessed.
Because of You, I am renewed.

Because of Your grace, I can meet You in the sky.
Because of Your love, I can live with You
In that glorious place
Where time never ends.

To purchase additional copies of:

GREEN PASTURE *Moments*

please contact:

Selah Publishing Group, LLC

Toll free 800-917-2665

or visit our website at

www.selahbooks.com